THE
RUTHLESS
ROMANS

TERRY DEARY

Illustrated by
Martin Brown

Hippo

For Dante Minghella,
a horrible historian, with thanks. TD

To Emily and Bella
(and Pink Teddy and Hippy). MB

218091 4

Scholastic Children's Books,
Euston House, 24 Eversholt Street,
London NW1 1DB, UK
A division of Scholastic Ltd
London ~ New York ~ Toronto ~ Sydney ~ Auckland
Mexico City ~ New Delhi ~ Hong Kong

Published in the UK by Scholastic Ltd, 2003

Text copyright © Terry Deary, 2003
Illustrations copyright © Martin Brown, 2003

10 digit ISBN 0 439 98237 5
13 digit ISBN 978 0439 98237 5

Typeset by M Rules
Printed in the UK by CPI Bookmarque, Croydon, CR0 4TD

14 16 18 20 19 17 15

CONTENTS

Horrible Histories:
The Savage Stone Age
The Awesome Egyptians
The Groovy Greeks
The Rotten Romans
The Cut-throat Celts
The Smashing Saxons
The Vicious Vikings
The Stormin' Normans
The Angry Aztecs
The Incredible Incas
The Measly Middle Ages
The Terrible Tudors
Even More Terrible Tudors
The Slimy Stuarts
The Gorgeous Georgians
The Vile Victorians
The Barmy British Empire
The Frightful First World War
The Woeful Second World War
The Blitzed Brits

Horrible Histories Specials:
Bloody Scotland
Cruel Kings and Mean Queens
Dark Knights and Dingy Castles
France
Ireland
Rowdy Revolutions
The 20th Century
The USA
Wicked Words

Also available:
Cruel Crimes and Painful Punishment
Dreadful Diary
Horrible Christmas
The Horribly Huge Quiz Book

INTRODUCTION

History has always been horrible. But some bits are more horrible than others. So, if there was a contest, who would be the most horrible people in history?

Of course, the Aztecs ripped out hearts because they thought that was the only way to make sure the sun would rise in the morning. They thought they had a good reason!

The Spanish torturers would have told you they were killing their victims – to make sure those victims could go to heaven. They thought they were helping!

Isn't it strange? Teachers and history books try to tell you how great the Roman Empire was…

Teachers often use the word 'civilized' to describe the Romans – that's the opposite to 'wild'.

Yet the Romans did something the heart-ripping Aztecs and the Spanish burners didn't do … they killed people for *fun*! The Romans made murder into a *sport*. They built wonderful buildings like the Colosseum, filled them with happy Romans and then massacred thousands of people and animals for *entertainment*.

They did lots of other ruthless and disgusting things too. Most history books (and teachers) try to forget the dark and deadly side of the ruthless Romans. What you need is a book that will tell you the *truth*. What you need is a *horrible* history of the ruthless Romans.

Now, I wonder where you'll find a book like that…

KILLER KINGS AND THE ROTTEN REPUBLIC

Rome's history is in three parts really...

- First there were Roman 'kings' – war leaders who went around smashing other people. Then the seventh king started smashing his own Roman people so...
- Kings were thrown out and the people ruled themselves – that's called a 'republic'. But the Romans decided one strong leader was better for smashing other people so...
- They created 'emperors' with an 'empire' which smashed everyone in sight ... and many who were out of sight too. It all started back in the distant mists of time in Italy...

Killer kings timeline

1000 BC Rome begins as a collection of villages on seven hilltops near the River Tiber. They are on the hilltops because it is easier to defend them against enemies all around.

753 BC Romulus – a reject from the nearby state of Alba Longa – murders his twin brother, Remus, then marks out a boundary. 'This is a new town and I name it after ... er, me!'

700 BC The seven villages all join together and build a meeting place – a 'forum' in one of the valleys between them – and the seven villages become one city.

673–642 BC Reign of Tullius Hostilius, third king of Rome. He sets about

attacking neighbours Alba Longa.

642–617 BC The fourth king, Ancus Marcius, makes the city bigger still, and builds the first bridge across the River Tiber. (That will come in *very* handy later for throwing people into the river.) He also builds Ostia at the mouth of that river to turn Rome into a seaport so the Romans can now massacre people on land *and* on the water.

616 BC Tarquinius Priscinus, becomes the fifth king of Rome. The Romans start to spread out and take over their local enemy city Alba Longa. Building starts on great temples and even greater sewers. (You can't make a big city without sewers.)

578–535 BC The sixth king, Servius Tullius, enlarges the city by building a wall around it, five miles long with 19 gates. (Lots of ways out when it comes to getting rid of the corpses of dead Romans later.) And Servius has the first Roman coins stamped with his head on them.

535–510 BC Reign of King Tarquin the Proud (posh name Tarquinius Superbus). Romans have now conquered about 350 square miles.

510 BC Wicked King Tarquin is thrown out of Rome and the city

8

picks its own leaders – it becomes a 'republic'. But some people think there was no such person as Tarquin the Proud! He was just a made-up man – a fairy tale to warn us about how evil kings can be.

Rotten Romulus and Remus

The legends say the terrible twins, Romulus and Remus, founded Rome in a wonderful (but wacky) way.

The boys were just babies in the state of Alba Longa when their wicked uncle decided to have them killed. They were put in a trough and thrown into the River Tiber.

Luckily the trough floated till it was caught on a thorny bush and they landed safely. The lads were cared for by a wolf and a woodpecker.

Then they were rescued and raised by a shepherd. When the brothers grew up they returned to the thorn bush to set up a city. Romulus ploughed a line around the city boundary. 'And don't you dare cross it, Remus,' he told his brother. So what did Remus do? Crossed it. What did Romulus do? Killed him. Problem solved.

Romulus was a bit short of women for his new city so he invited the Sabine people to a party – and captured all their women for his men to marry. Another problem solved.

In the end Romulus disappeared in a storm – and became a god!

Believe all that and you need a Roman woodpecker to peck some sense into your wooden head! But…

Did you know…?
The story of Romulus and Remus was *not* the story the Romans usually told their children about the making of Rome. The Romans liked to believe that the first Romans came from near Greece, after the battle of Troy.

You remember that tale? Where the Trojans were beaten by a wooden horse full of Greek soldiers (and probably a few Greek woodpeckers)? Well, some Trojans escaped. They were led into Italy by the hero, Aeneas, and they ended up starting the towns that became Rome.

The Romans simply invented a list of kings and said, 'This is our history!' Which just goes to show – you can never trust a history book. Except a *Horrible Histories* book, of course.

The rotten republic

After the Romans threw out King Tarquin in 510 BC they really began spreading out around the world. Of course the people the Romans conquered didn't *want* to be conquered. There were lots of bloody battles and bad feelings. The Romans usually won because they were more ruthless than their enemies. They even practised being bloodthirsty by slaughtering people in Rome – for fun.

Rotten republic timeline

390 BC The Gauls (from France) invade Rome and wreck most of the houses and temples. So the Romans build a city wall. Sensible. It will mark the boundary for the next 600 years.

295 BC Decius Mus wins a battle for the Romans that makes them lords of Italy. Now there's just the rest of the world to go out and grab.

264–231 BC Rome at war against Carthage (North Africa). Romans need to learn how to fight at sea as well as on land.

218 BC Rome at war with Carthage again – they are stuffed by Hannibal at Trasimene and then Cannae. In 202 BC they finally beat Hannibal. Who can stop them now?

146 BC The Romans destroy the Greek city of Corinth and destroy the ancient Greek fighting spirit. Glorious Greece becomes part of rotten Rome. The Mediterranean Sea is starting to look like a Roman lake – they own everything around it.

132 BC Tiberius Gracchus tries to change the way Rome is run – take power from the rich and give land to the poor. The rich are not happy so they murder Gracchus. Murdering Roman leaders will now become a

Roman hobby. Gracchus' brother fails with the same plan and kills himself – another Roman hobby.

82 BC Romans are squabbling among themselves. Sulla marches in with an army, massacres anyone who is against him, and takes over as a dictator. The beginning of the end for the republic.

73 BC Gladiators revolt, led by super Spartacus, and rampage around Italy. But they never manage to capture Rome. They are finally defeated and crucified. Roman Crassus is the hero and becomes the new top Roman with General Pompey.

55 BC Superstar general Julius Caesar smashes Gaul and crosses into Germany and Britain. He's a great man, popular with the people. Then Crassus dies in battle with the Parthians. That leaves just Julius and Pompey as top dogs.

49 BC Pompey (back in Rome) tells Julius Caesar (up in Gaul), 'I will let you help me rule Rome – *if* you come back and leave your army behind.' Julius doesn't trust him. He refuses to come quietly and arrives in Rome with his army. Pompey runs away. It is the start of 19 years of Romans fighting Romans.

46 BC Julius Caesar wins power and has a party – a death party. Hundreds of gladiator fights and animal hunts in the arena. He says they are funeral fights, in memory of his daughter – though she died *eight years* earlier! But republics only work when people agree: 'Winners rule OK'. The Roman republic fell apart because there were too many *really* bad losers who said: 'Winners die OK'. Losers turned into rebels, killed the winners and became the winners. So other losers killed the new winners … and, oh, you can see how it goes on…

44 BC Caesar's just too powerful. He is stabbed to death by worried enemies. Caesar's nephew Octavian and his old friend Mark Antony will share power for a while but sooner or later they will fight one another, won't they?

31 BC Octavian declares war on Mark Antony's girlfriend Cleopatra, Queen of Egypt. Narked Mark has to fight for her. He's beaten and kills himself. Octavian top dog now and…

27 BC …Rome (which hates having a king) makes Octavian 'Emperor'. He changes his name to 'Augustus'. End of the 'republic' – but really it's been finished for 50 years – and start of the 'empire'.

SUPER SUPERSTITIONS AND QUAINT CUSTOMS

The Romans had dozens of gods. You've probably had to learn some of them in school and know the usual boring ones: Neptune – god of the sea, Jupiter – chief god ... that sort of thing. But there were Roman gods that even your teacher has never heard of. It may be useful to call on one of these gods at the right moment! These may look weird, wacky and made-up, but they are true...

Horrible Histories **top five gods and goddesses**

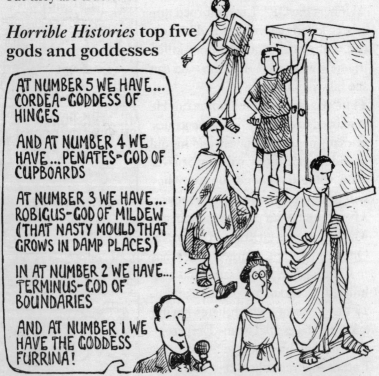

AT NUMBER 5 WE HAVE... CORDEA-GODDESS OF HINGES

AND AT NUMBER 4 WE HAVE...PENATES-GOD OF CUPBOARDS

AT NUMBER 3 WE HAVE... ROBIGUS-GOD OF MILDEW (THAT NASTY MOULD THAT GROWS IN DAMP PLACES)

IN AT NUMBER 2 WE HAVE... TERMINUS-GOD OF BOUNDARIES

AND AT NUMBER 1 WE HAVE THE GODDESS FURRINA!

Furrina's festival was celebrated every 25 July, but by 100 BC no one could remember what she was goddess of!

14

So there you have it! On 25 July let's all have a party. A party for anything you like, and Furrina can be your goddess! Have a party for your hamster – Furrina can be the goddess of furry things. Have a party for the end of term – Furrina is the goddess of school holidays! Furrina is the greatest goddess of all because she's the goddess of whatever you want her to be!

Act like a Roman

Fancy being a Roman priest? Then here's what you do…

Whipping people was part of a ceremony called the 'Lupercalia' – on 15 February each year. This would persuade the gods to bring you good crops and large herds of animals the following summer. Sometimes the Romans sacrificed dogs at the Lupercalia.

Did you know…?
In October the winning horse in a chariot race was sacrificed. The tail, dripping blood, was used to bless the crops. Different districts of Rome had a competition to see which one could have the biggest prize – the horse's head.

Awesome augury

'Augury' was the Roman name for fortune-telling – looking into the future. The Romans were so superstitious they had an augury 'kit' that they took with them into battle.

You may want to look into the future yourself. If so then why not try the Roman augury method. This will allow you to…

- Check your exam results before you even take the tests. (See if it's worth even going to school!)
- Find out if it's a good time to ask your parents for a pocket-money rise. (Or will you have to wash Dad's car … again?)

- See if your football team will win on Saturday. (Or should you save your ticket money and stay in bed?)

Here's how to augur…

Augur away

You need:
Sacred chickens. [Chickens from your local butcher aren't good enough. They have to be living chickens. If they're not holy chickens then take them to your local temple and have the vicar sprinkle them with holy water.]
Some cake with seeds on top.

To augur:
1 Feed small pieces of the cake to the sacred chickens.
2 Watch the chickens eat the cake.

The meaning:
If the chickens eat the cake and bits of seed fall out of their beaks then this is a good sign. Today whatever you do will be lucky.

But if the chickens refuse to eat the cake then this is a bad sign. Do not go into battle / school / hysterics. Stay in bed and pray the gods don't send a thunderbolt to get you while you are lying there.

Of course, the Romans knew that the sacred chickens were messengers of the gods. Roman admiral Claudius Pulcher saw chickens refuse to eat before a sea battle with Carthage.

17

He threw the chickens overboard saying he didn't believe their message of doom, but the chickens had the last laugh – or at least the last cluck. The Romans lost 93 ships and the battle.

Wonderful weddings

Romans often used fortune-telling as part of their wedding ceremonies. A posh Roman service included prayers and a bloodless sacrifice (roasting a cabbage and offering it to a god). Guests would also eat holy bread, and the bride and groom would sit in two chairs that were tied together and covered in lamb-skin.

What other way could you be married in ancient Rome – especially if you weren't posh and couldn't afford the holy bread and priests and all that?

a) Just agreeing, 'We are married … OK?'.

b) Living together for a year – so long as the wife isn't away from home for more than three days.

c) Agreeing to be married in front of five people and someone holding a pair of scales.

Answer: All of them.

18

Batty beliefs

Would you walk under a ladder? A lot of people today believe that will bring them bad luck. (It would if the ladder was attached to a fire-engine speeding towards you at 60 miles an hour.) Here are a few strange superstitions – but which did Romans believe? Answer true or false…

1 It is bad luck to enter a house left-foot first.
2 Sausages should be banned.
3 It is lucky to have a cow on the roof of your house.

4 Women should comb their hair with the spear of a dead man for luck.
5 Dead people can become ghosts.
6 If a man dreams of being a gladiator he will marry a rich woman.
7 The birthday of Emperor Tiberius' sister-in-law is a lucky day in Rome.
8 Animals should only be sacrificed after they ask for it.
9 Crows are lucky.
10 A lightning strike is caused by angry gods so you should sacrifice four enemies to keep the gods happy.

Answers:

1 True. Rich Romans put a servant at the door to make sure everyone entered right-foot first. That's where we get the name 'footman' for a servant.

2 True. Sausages were banned in Rome by Emperor Constantine. They were eaten at barbarian festivals and Constantine didn't want Romans mixed up with those dreadful people.

3 False. They believed it was *un*lucky. In 191 BC, two cows climbed on to the roof of a Roman house. The city priests said this was a bad sign. They ordered the cattle to be burned alive and their ashes to be scattered on the River Tiber.

4 True. The man should have been killed in the arena – the fresher the better.

5 True. A murdered person would haunt the world, hoping to take revenge on their murderer.

6 True. The bad news is the rich woman you married would be sly and big-headed.

7 False. Tiberius hated Agrippina and sent her to Pandataria Island where she starved herself to death. The Emperor made her birthday one of Rome's days of bad luck.

8 True. The animal that went for the chop had to show it wanted to die. How? By stretching its neck out for the axe. Could the Romans cheat and get the animal to stretch its neck out? You bet!

9 False. Crows were an unlucky sign. Ruthless Roman rebel Sejanus was surrounded by cawing crows that then went off to settle on the prison roof. Sejanus should have seen it as a sign. Shortly after he was arrested and executed. He was surprised by the arrest. But the crows had tried to warn him!

10 True. In 228 BC the lightning scared the Romans gathered in the forum and a fortune teller said there was only one way to stop it happening again – sacrifice two couples of enemy tribespeople. They buried two Celts and two Greeks alive under the forum. They could still be there to this day!

Cruel curses

The Romans believed you could curse your enemies and bring them bad luck. It may be true! Why not try it? Here's what to do...

1 Write down the name of a dead person – their ghost will do the dirty work.
2 Write down who you want to curse.
3 Write down what you want to happen.
Here is an example...

Dear Julius Caesar,
Please curse Mrs Popplewick of 5 Willow Way, Walberswick, for telling my mum I bounced my football off her nice clean car. I had to clean the whole car again thanks to pooey Popplewick. May the hair on her chin turn into a big bushy beard! Thank you, Mr Caesar.

Henry Hooligan

4 Take your curse to the nearest well and drop it down.
5 Wait and see what happens.

Grim ghosts

When Emperor Caligula died his body was burned in his garden … but not completely. What was left was buried, but the garden became haunted. Caligula's sisters had the remains dug up and burned to complete ashes. The ghost never returned.

That was just one of many ghost stories the Romans told. A Roman called Pliny wrote a letter in which he told another ghost story. A ghost told his friend, Athenodorus, where to find his corpse…

ATHENODORUS ROSE FROM HIS BED AND WENT OUT OF THE DOOR. THE GARDEN WAS LIT BY A HALF MOON AND THE GHOSTLY SHAPE WAS CLEARER THERE. IT WAS THE SHAPE OF A SMALL MAN AND HIS HEAD SEEMED TO DRIP BLOOD. THE HIDEOUS CREATURE POINTED TO A SPOT BETWEEN THE WALL AND THE SUNDIAL AND SAID, 'DIG THERE AND FIND MY MURDERED BODY. GIVE ME A TRUE ROMAN BURIAL SO MY SPIRIT MAY REST.'

ATHENODORUS MOVED TOWARDS THE SPOT AND THE GHOSTLY FIGURE VANISHED. NEXT MORNING HE HAD SLAVES DIG WHERE THE GHOST TOLD HIM AND THEY CAME ACROSS A BODY IN A BLOOD-STAINED SHEET. IT WAS ALMOST ROTTED TO A SKELETON. THEY RAISED IT AND TOOK IT OUTSIDE OF THE CITY TO A CEMETERY AND GAVE IT A BURIAL. SINCE THAT DAY ATHENODORUS HAS NOT BEEN TROUBLED BY THE GHOST.

You may not believe the ghost story, but most Romans would have believed it. For the Romans, it was important to bury friends properly. Criminals could be torn apart in the arena by wild animals, but that was only part of their punishment. The other part was to have their corpses dumped without a funeral, which meant they would *never* get to the Roman heaven. Maybe those thousands of victims are still wandering the Earth, crying, 'Help! Help! I've been eaten by a crocodile!' Spooky or what?

Heavenly horrors

The Romans believed that after you died you went to a place called the Underworld. You crossed the River Styx on a ferry and went to a happier place. But if your corpse hadn't been properly buried then the ferryman, Charon, would not let you cross. Your corpse just lay on the banks of the river till dogs came to eat it.

A Roman writer told a story of a man who went to the Underworld and saw the unburied dead scattered around. The 'Furies' – vicious 'avenging angels' – hung around there and enjoyed the hideous sights:

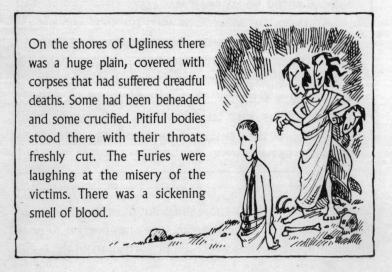

On the shores of Ugliness there was a huge plain, covered with corpses that had suffered dreadful deaths. Some had been beheaded and some crucified. Pitiful bodies stood there with their throats freshly cut. The Furies were laughing at the misery of the victims. There was a sickening smell of blood.

GORY GLADIATORS

Gladiators were men (and sometimes women) who fought in front of an audience – a bit like some footballers today. But footballers aren't given swords and spears and nets to fight with. Though it's a nice idea…

Most gladiator fights stopped when one fighter was too wounded or exhausted to go on. But some of the fights went on till one of the gladiators was dead. Where on earth did the Romans get this gruesome idea from?

Like a lot of their ideas, it was probably pinched. (The Romans pinched their religion, letters and writing, and theatre from the Greeks, for example. They even stole complete Greek temples and shipped them over to Rome.)

They nicked the public-killing idea from the Etruscan people who once ruled the Romans. These Etruscans lived just to the north and ruled Rome in the early days. The Etruscans could be pretty nasty. In 356 BC they sacrificed 307 Roman prisoners in the centre of the city. (And the Etruscans possibly 'borrowed' *their* ideas from the Greeks.)

This gladiator thing all started at funerals. Nowadays a funeral means a few words from the vicar followed by tea and sandwiches. The Etruscan funerals didn't have tea or sandwiches – they just murdered one of their enemies over the grave. It was revenge, and it was a gift to the dead man.

If the dead man *was* happy in heaven then he wouldn't come back to haunt the living. So funeral killers were the first ghost-busters.

But, did you know that sometimes the Etruscans killed a puppet instead of a living human?

Then the Etruscans thought of a new idea – it was much more exciting. Take TWO prisoners (or slaves or criminals) and let them fight each other at the grave. Call them 'gladiators'. The loser becomes the sacrifice to the dead person.

To make the contest even more exciting the gladiators were trained to fight in special gladiator schools – watching skilled fighters was more interesting than watching two men with swords just chop at one another.

Romans began to ask for gladiator fights *before* they died.

One man, Sestillius, wrote in his will…

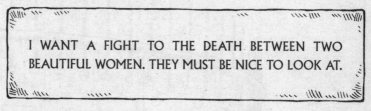

I WANT A FIGHT TO THE DEATH BETWEEN TWO BEAUTIFUL WOMEN. THEY MUST BE NICE TO LOOK AT.

Another, Messinus, wrote a will which said…

In life I loved the company of two young slaves, Marcus and Tarquin. I want them to fight to the death over my grave.

GEE THANKS, BOSS

Messinus *didn't* get his wish. The Romans felt sorry for the boys and stopped it.

But the Romans weren't always so kind. In Pollentia a man was going to be buried *without* a gladiator fight at the funeral. So the people of the town stopped the funeral and wouldn't let the family bury him till they had paid for a gladiator fight. Nasty. And things got nastier…

In the year 264 BC, a Roman called Brutus Pera had *three* gladiator fights at his funeral. And they were moved out of the graveyard and into the cattle market so everyone could get a good view. The contests became bigger and bigger.

By 216 BC there were 22 fights going on at a single funeral.

In 174 BC, a chap called Flamininus had a great funeral for his dead dad: it went on for three days and involved 74 gladiators. Would you do that for your dad?

Killer Colosseum

At first gladiator games were held in any open spaces – marketplaces, forums or fields. But by around 100 BC people were building special arenas. The greatest killing ground of all was the Colosseum in Rome. It held 50,000 people and it was opened in AD 80.

Easy question: Why was it called the 'Colosseum'?

Answer: Because it was built near the colossal statue of Emperor Nero.

Very hard question: Why were its large columns *cemented* together? They were supposed to be pinned with big iron pins but…

a) Romans kept pinching the pins.

b) The pins went rusty and the building almost fell down before it was finished.

c) The gladiators needed the pins to make enough swords to slaughter all the animals.

Answer: **a)** You can't trust anyone, can you?

Did you know…?

The Colosseum was the size of a modern football stadium – and that was *small*! The Circus Maximus was *twelve* times bigger than the Colosseum, and would hold a quarter of a million people – that's a quarter of all the people in Rome.

The Romans packed the Circus Maximus to watch chariot races. It was more popular than the Colosseum because men and women could sit together there – that wasn't allowed in the Colosseum.

Crushing defeat

The Colosseum was fairly safe because it was built of stone. But some earlier arenas were definitely *not* safe – or as safe as a hedgehog on a motorway. A writer called Tacitus described one…

At Fidenae there was an accident that killed as many as a great war. It began and ended in a moment. An ex-slave, Atilius, built an arena for gladiator shows. But he didn't build it on solid ground and he didn't fasten the wooden platforms together very firmly. He only built it to make some easy money. Fans flocked in – men and women of all ages – because there had been very few good shows in the reign of Emperor Tiberius. The packed building collapsed, inwards and outwards, crushing or smothering a huge crowd.

Tacitus went on to say the dead were the lucky ones – it was worse for the mangled fans who knew their loved ones were trapped somewhere in the mess of wood and bodies.

In the daytime they could see them – at night they could hear their screams and moans. When the ruins were cleared people rushed in to kiss and hug the corpses of their families. They even argued over bodies that were so smashed they weren't sure whose they were. Fifty thousand were killed or injured.

The crowds had rushed in to see blood in the arena, and they certainly saw it.

Emperor Caligula did *not* have a big arena collapse in his time. He said…

What a shame – it must be interesting to watch!

Not from the bottom of the heap, Caligula.

Did you know…?
Games were usually fought on sand. But emperors Caligula and Nero liked coloured dust instead. They mixed white and greenish-blue dust with red dust. A pretty place to die.

Scrapping spectators

One of the first arenas was built in Pompeii in around 80 BC. It held 20,000 people – a lot for a fairly small town. How did they fill it? With people from other towns in the region. And that's how the trouble started.

People came in from the town of Nuceria – and the people of Nuceria hated the people of Pompeii, just like some rival football fans still do today. The Nucerians wrote nasty graffiti on the walls of Pompeii and probably enjoyed threatening their rivals. Tacitus described what happened next...

It was the sort of deadly riot that you could still imagine happening at a football ground today, sadly. In Rome the emperor was horrified to hear what had happened. What would *you* do if you were emperor after such a murderous riot?

a) Invite the people of Pompeii and Nuceria to fight in Rome.

b) Ban all games in Pompeii for ten years.

c) Have the Pompeii arena pulled down.

> *Answer:* The shocked emperor did **b)**.

Prezzies for the plebs

The posh people in Rome were the 'patricians'; the workers were the 'plebeians' (or plebs for short). The patricians may have ruled the country, but they needed to keep the plebs happy. So the patricians gave the plebs the bloody arena games, they gave them food and they gave them gifts. The rich often gave out gifts at New Year.

In Roman Alexandria a rich man paraded a wagon through the streets with a model of a cave built on it. Doves were released from the cave with long ribbons tied to their feet. The poor could grab a ribbon to catch a dove – and eat it!

The greatest of the gift-givers was usually the emperor. At the arena some would give out lottery tickets with prizes for the lucky ones. Emperor Elagabalus gave out slips of paper with the prizes written on them...

There were slaves and even houses to be won. No wonder people were trampled to death as they scrambled to get one of Elagabalus' bits of paper.

But Elagabalus had a nasty sense of humour. Some of the prizes were *not* what you'd like to win in your school raffle.

Lies my teacher told

Teachers learn from other teachers and from books. But sometimes they get their facts wrong because some books are wrong. But, as this is a *Horrible Histories* book, you can at last hear the truth.

1 Gladiator deaths

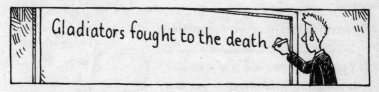

Gladiators fought to the death

Oh no they didn't. Not all of them anyway.

Proper gladiators cost a lot of money to feed and train. Posh Romans paid the bills and put on gladiator shows for the poor Romans. In return, the poor Romans voted for them. No one would spend all that money to see it wasted with a few short, sharp chops. In fact, the top gladiators fought like today's boxers – the crowds loved watching their skill and betting on who would win. Those top gladiators lived to fight again.

Roman noble Cicero wrote to a friend...

> What fine gladiators you have bought. If you had rented them out you could have got your money back on just those two shows.

So, gladiators were groups of entertainers, bought by the rich for free shows or to be hired out. Gladiators were *not* cheap slaves to be wasted in the arena.

Criminals *were* sent in to the arena to fight till they died. They dressed like gladiators but the Romans knew they were not the real thing. Those criminals (called 'noxii') gave the Romans all the blood and death they wanted. Prisoners of war were also sent to the arena just to be slaughtered.

Noxii were badly trained, and had little chance of winning. Even if they did win they fought on until someone beat them. But the real gladiators fought for years and many won their freedom after giving the crowds lots of fighting fun. Emperor Tiberius even complained:

> *I had to pay one old, free gladiator a thousand gold pieces to get him back into the arena!*

Did you know...?
Emperor Caligula liked to have people executed and then sell off all they had owned. Sometimes Caligula held an auction and he did the selling. If you wanted to buy something you just had to nod your head. One old senator, Aponius, fell asleep and his head kept nodding. When he woke up he found he had bought 13 gladiators ... and they cost him 90,000 gold pieces!

2 Gladiator salute

Gladiators who entered the arena cried to the emperor:
'We who are about to die salute you'

Oh no they didn't. This happened only *once*. And the dying men were *not* gladiators. They were criminals who were put in a mock sea battle. They had to kill each other to entertain Emperor Claudius. They cried out 'We salute you' in the hope that the Emperor would spare their lives. He said, 'Get on with it.'

At first they refused to fight. The Emperor threatened them: 'Fight or my guards will burn and hack you to death!' Then they tried to fight without hurting each other too much. Again they were told to fight properly or die.

The criminals began to really fight. The Emperor enjoyed it and spared the lives of the ones who survived.

Glad-iator to meet you

The Roman poet Ovid said the arena was a very good place to meet women. How can you chat one up? Just turn to them and ask…

These programmes were sold in the streets and in the arenas – just like programmes at football matches today. To be honest, you didn't have to have a printed programme.

The programme was usually the same…

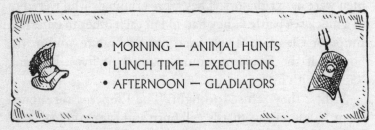

- MORNING — ANIMAL HUNTS
- LUNCH TIME — EXECUTIONS
- AFTERNOON — GLADIATORS

Plus there were heralds who entered the arena and shouted out the names of the fighters or the criminals, and servants carrying banners into the arena with the names on.

THREE GLADIATORS FROM GAUL FIGHTING THREE GLADIATORS FROM THRACE

HELLO MUM

There were also adverts for the arena games painted by roadsides. If there wasn't a wall handy then the painter would paint the latest gladiator news on a gravestone!

See the best gladiators win! the REST are IN PEACEs!

Fighting fellers

There were several types of gladiators – it would be boring if they were all dressed and armed the same way. Here are the main ones:

ANDABATAE
Fought blindfolded – very funny for the audience.

DIMACHERI
Fought with two swords – slick slicers.

RETIARII
Fought with nets and a trident – a bit fishy that.

HOPLOMACHI
Fought in a suit of armour – hot work.

LAQUEATORES
Fought with a rope – no noose was bad news for them.

SECUTORES
Fought with sword and shield – they were lucky ones.

SAGITTARII
*Fought with bows and arrows –
hoping for an arrow escape.*

BESTIARII
*Fought with anything against
wild animals – beastly.*

BUT one sort of gladiator you won't hear about in school books were the 'scissores'. The word means 'carvers'. Why will you not see a picture of 'scissores' in your school books?

a) They didn't exist (I just made them up).

b) 'Scissores' were dressmakers who fought with scissors in the street, not the arena.

c) No one knows anything about them except for their name.

Answer: **c)** The name 'scissores' is carved on a stone in a list of gladiators. But no one knows what they did. So here, for the first time, is an image of what we think this fiendish fighter may have looked like…

Freedom fighters

Most gladiators were slaves, but some freemen chose to become gladiators. If they did well they could retire rich. Gladiator Publius Ostorius was a freeman and had 51 fights.

40

But he had to give up his freedom. He had to sign a contract before he entered gladiator school. Would you sign this for the pleasure of going to school…?

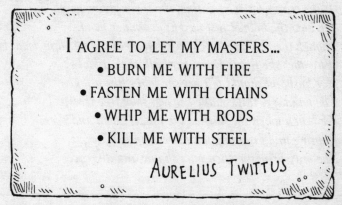

I AGREE TO LET MY MASTERS...
• BURN ME WITH FIRE
• FASTEN ME WITH CHAINS
• WHIP ME WITH RODS
• KILL ME WITH STEEL

AURELIUS TWITTUS

The only way out was to buy yourself out. One Roman story tells of a girl who bought her brother out of gladiator school – but he went back. So she bought him out again … and again … and again. In the end she waited till he was asleep and cut off his thumb so he could never hold a sword and never fight again. The gladiator wanted revenge in court…

I WANT HER THUMB CUT OFF TOO

Wild women

Women sometimes fought as gladiators. But many men were shocked at the idea. The Roman poet Juvenal wrote a very nasty poem about female gladiators. He said they were not only a disgrace to their husbands – they were also just a joke as fighters…

The Gorgeous Gladiators by Juvenal

See how she slashes at dummies of wood,
As she trains for the fighting, she is simply no good.
See how the helmet just weighs down her head,
Though there's really no chance that she'll end up plain dead.
Why does she fight? Does she think she's a bloke?
Her husband should tell her she looks like a joke.
The bandages thick make her legs look like trees,
We laugh when she rests as she squats down and pees.
Panting and groaning with sweat on her face,
She only brings women pure shame and disgrace.

In 200 AD, Emperor Septimius Severus agreed with Juvenal. He banned women from fighting in the arena … but, he said, it was still OK to throw them in to be torn apart by wild animals, of course.

Cheating chaps

Gladiators were supposed to fight hard and put on a good show for the audience. But one group shocked Emperor Caligula when they refused to fight. Here's what happened…

A GROUP OF RETIARII ENTERED THE ARENA…

THEN THEIR OPPONENTS, SECUTORES, ENTERED…

43

Caligula called it 'murder' and he probably had the Retiarii executed anyway. But at least they must have had a bit of a chuckle before they died!

A dreadful way to die

Not all criminals wanted to die in front of a screaming crowd of Romans. Some killed themselves before they entered the arena. But that wasn't easy because criminals sentenced to fight to the death were guarded day and night. The only time they had to themselves was in the toilet.

In the toilet there were sticks with sponges on the end. These were dipped in water and used instead of toilet paper – get the picture? Everyone used the same sponges and rinsed them after they used them.

A German prisoner of war was due to go in the arena and said, 'I want to use the toilet before I go in.' The guard allowed him to go.

The German took the toilet sponge and pushed it down his throat till the sharp stick had killed him.

Other criminals were known to kill themselves by leaning over the side of the cart that took them to the games. If they could stick their head in the spokes of the cartwheel it would crush their skull as it turned. Around AD 390, 29 Saxons strangled each other rather than fight.

Bopped bodies

It was no use faking a fight. If you were meant to die in the arena the Romans made sure you did. How? Two men came into the arena after your fight. One was dressed in a tight tunic, wore soft leather boots and a mask that gave him the nose of a hawk. He carried a big hammer.

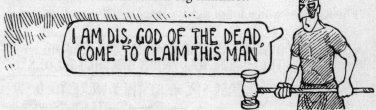

In front of Dis was another man with wings on his helmet and carrying a red-hot poker...

Mercury stuck his red-hot poker into you to make sure you weren't just pretending to be dead, then Dis made absolutely sure by smashing you very hard on the forehead. Then slaves came and carried you off on a stretcher. It was a bit like a football match today ... at least that very small bit with the stretcher is.

But if you were a criminal who had been executed in the arena then hooks were stuck in your body and you were dragged out – and that doesn't happen to footballers today. (Not even footballers in Rome.)

RUTHLESS ROMAN ARMY

The Romans won a lot of fights. Teacher tells you they had…

DISCIPLINE! THE ROMAN SOLDIERS DID WHAT THEY WERE TOLD! WHAT DID THEY DO, DEREK?

PLEASE, SIR, WHAT THEY WERE TOLD, SIR!

And they had good stabbing swords and armour and … zzzz! Excuse us while we fall asleep. Never mind the armour and the weapons. What you really want to know is that they were *ruthless*. They were nasty, cruel and vicious. *That's* why they won.

If you are a soldier and you surrender, you might expect your enemy to spare your life. Not if the enemy was a Roman. And the Romans didn't just kill their prisoners – they took them back to Rome and killed them in the city centre so the rest of the Romans could watch.

Doggy disaster

When the Romans captured New Carthage in Spain in 202 BC their general, Scipio, gave the order…

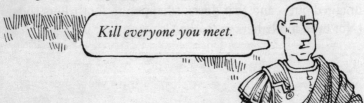

Kill everyone you meet.

The soldiers did more than that – they cut the legs off animals and chopped dogs in two. Picture it: chopped chows to the left, poodle pieces to the right and halved hounds h'everywhere.

TRUST DAMIEN HIRSTUS TO SHOW OFF!

Evil to enemies

In AD 70, the Romans wanted to capture Jerusalem but the Jewish defenders refused to surrender. The Romans had thousands of Jewish prisoners. Every day the Romans crucified 500 of those prisoners outside the walls of the city so their friends could watch them die in agony. And this went on for several months!

If a Roman soldier was really kind he'd break the legs of the victim nailed to the cross – that way the crucified person would die in a couple of hours. But the Roman soldiers could often be extra cruel to people they didn't like and they could keep them alive on the cross for two or three days so the suffering went on and on.

Death for deserters

If you ran away from a battle then the Romans would probably execute you. But if your whole legion ran away they couldn't execute you *all*, could they? Sometimes.

- In AD 214, 370 men were thrown from the Tarpeian Rock in Rome for deserting.
- In that year a Roman commander captured 2,000 deserters in Sicily and beheaded every one.

- In 146 BC, cruel General Scipio crucified runaways from his army.
- But cruellest of all, in 167 BC, the Roman leader Lucius Aemilius Paullus laid a group of deserters down on the ground – and had them *trampled by elephants*.

More often, a troop of cowards were 'decimated' – which meant having one soldier in every ten killed. The survivors were sent back into battle. Emperor Augustus made the nine 'lucky' soldiers club their 'unlucky' friend to death.

Soldiers didn't even have to run away to get this treatment. Crassus had 500 soldiers out of 5,000 decimated when their only 'crime' was to lose in battle to Spartacus and his gladiator rebels. Don't blame the general – blame the soldiers.

Imagine decimating football teams if they lost!

Ruthless to rebels

Some Roman soldiers who rebelled against Rome were executed in an odd way. In 270 BC over 300 troops rebelled and were marched back to Rome. They were tied to stakes and whipped till they were half dead. Then they were finished off by having the backs of their necks chopped with an axe. They weren't beheaded completely – maybe that would leave too many bits to pick up?

Whips for winners

Romans loved a winner. If a general's army killed 5,000 of the enemy in battle, he was given a parade through Rome. The men got their share of the captured loot and marched to the temple of Jupiter. Jupiter's statue has a red face – and the Roman general's face was painted red to match. (That must have looked dreadful with the purple and gold robes he was given for the day.) Then, to remind him not to get too big-headed, there was a whip attached to his chariot – that's what Rome would use on him if he misbehaved. Just to round off the party a defeated enemy general was put to death. Nice.

Tricky tactics

The Roman army won a lot of wars because they were just too clever for the enemy. In 396 BC they had been trying for ten years to get into the city of Veii, north of Rome, where their Etruscan enemies were holding out. At last General Furius Camillus came up with a cunning plot to enter the city. If he'd written a report back to the senate it may have looked like this…

SIRS,
VEII IS TAKEN. FOR YEARS WE HAVE FAILED TO ATTACK UP THE HILL TO THE CITY, SO I DECIDED TO DIG THROUGH THE HILL. MY MEN DUG A TUNNEL RIGHT UP TO THEIR TEMPLE OF JUNO. WE COULD HEAR THEIR KING OFFERING A SACRIFICE.

WE BROKE THROUGH AND AFTER FIERCE FIGHTING WE OVERCAME THE PEOPLE OF VEII. WOMEN AND SLAVES WERE HURLING STONES DOWN ON OUR MEN FROM THE ROOFTOPS. WE SET FIRE TO THE HOUSES AND THEY WERE BURNED ALIVE FOR THEIR CHEEK.

OUR VICTORIOUS TROOPS ARE RETURNING TO ROME. I LOOK FORWARD TO A GLORIOUS WELCOME.

FURIUS CAMILLIUS

But the reply was not at all what he expected.

FURIUS CAMILLUS,
REPORTS HAVE REACHED US THAT THERE WAS GREAT WEALTH IN VEII AND THAT YOU HAVE TAKEN A LARGE SHARE OF IT FOR YOURSELF. AS YOU KNOW, ALL LOOT COMES TO ROME FIRST. THE SENATE HAS DECIDED TODAY TO HAVE YOU EXILED.

ALL GOOD WISHES,

SECRETARY TO THE SENATE

Poor old Furius! (A lot of other popular history books would say, 'Bet he was furious!' But this is a *Horrible Histories* book and we don't have awful jokes like that … much.) Furius had the last laugh, though. When the Gauls attacked, in 390 BC, the Romans had to call him back to help them.

EVIL ENEMIES

Why were the Romans so ruthless? Maybe they had to be, because their enemies could be pretty rotten to Romans when the Romans lost. And the Romans didn't always win.

Mind you, when they lost it wasn't always the savage enemies that beat them – sometimes it was their own stupid leaders! In 217 BC Hannibal's army from Carthage was helped by the weather – and by a very careless Roman general…

THE ROMAN TIMES

HORRIBLE HANNIBAL LASHES LEGIONS

Harmful Hannibal

The Roman army has suffered a dreadful defeat at the hands of Hannibal and his Carthage cutthroats. Hannibal was being chased right back to Carthage by our bold boys and hid in the hills above Lake Trasimene. He knew the Romans were on his tail and he planned an awful ambush.

Roman general Flaminius led his legions along the shore of the lake but fat-head Flaminius didn't send scouts on ahead. So he had no idea what was waiting round the corner.

The crafty Carthage men were helped by a foul fog that

floated over the lake and hid Hannibal's army. When they rushed down from the hills our legions were driven into the lake. Many of our soggy soldiers sank and drowned. We have lost four legions and Hannibal is now heading for Rome itself.

Tragic Trasimene

It's a bad day for the Roman people – and we all know who to blame.

Worse was still to come. The Romans lost the next big battle with Hannibal at Cannae in 216 BC. Hannibal's African army slaughtered them. But he never went on to take the city of Rome. In the end, the Romans raised new armies, defeated Carthage and destroyed the city completely – they even sowed the fields with salt so nothing could grow there.

Burning Sulla

The Romans believed it was best to bury their dead heroes in graves. Then word reached Rome that their enemies were digging up the corpses and scattering them around. So the Roman general Sulla started a new fashion – cremation…

WHEN I DIE I DON'T WANT PEOPLE DIGGING ME UP IN REVENGE. BURN MY BODY PLEASE

He died in 78 BC and they followed his wishes so he became the first important Roman to be cremated.

Nasty for Numidia

The Roman armies really enjoyed taking captured enemies back to Rome and showing them to the Roman people. Enemy leaders were flogged then dragged with nooses around their necks to the forum. Then they were executed and that was an excuse for the Romans to have lots of parties.

Numidia in North Africa was ruled by Jugurtha – who thought he was better than the Romans. He murdered his enemies, who happened to be friends of the Romans, and the Romans were not very pleased with him. In 110 BC he drove the Romans out of Numidia. It was time for them to get ruthless.

In 105 BC the Romans invited him to Rome to explain himself to the senate – a bit like you being called to see the head teacher! (Why was Jugurtha daft enough to go to Rome? Because his wife's dad said he would be safe.)

Jugurtha said…

The senate said, 'Fine! But, before you go, we have a parade arranged for you.'

Then the ruthless Romans led Jugurtha through the streets of Rome. But there was a nasty surprise waiting for him at the end of the parade. His clothes and jewels were torn off him, and when his ear-ring was torn off it took half his ear with it. Then Jugurtha was thrown into a cold prison cell. The shock drove him mad and he died after six days from cold and starvation.

Laugh with the lions

When the Megarians from Greece attacked the Roman army of Julius Caesar they used a secret weapon – lions that had been trained to eat victims in the arenas.

The Megarians set the lions on to the Romans – but the lions turned round and attacked the Megarians instead! (Maybe Megarians taste better than Romans!) The Roman soldiers must have had a bit of a laugh that day.

Cut-throat Celts?

The Celts liked to collect the heads of their enemies. They put them on show and boasted about how they had killed them. But did you know that it wasn't only the Celts who had this horrible hobby. The Romans soon copied the cruel Celt collectors...

- From 87 BC the Romans were quite keen on collecting heads. A top Roman official, Consul Octavius, was beheaded that year and his head shown in the forum. Many senator heads followed and the Romans became head-hunters, carrying the heads of defeated enemies back to Rome.

- In 43 BC Roman troops cut off the head of Trebonius who was one of Caesar's murderers. They threw and kicked the head across the pavements till it was smashed to pieces.

- Old Galba was emperor for just nine months before he was assassinated in Rome. His head was carried round the city on the end of a spear. His servant rescued it and buried it with his body.

- Galba's supporters got the head treatment, too. The Greek historian Plutarch wrote…

> The dead bodies of Galba's friends were scattered all over the forum. And, as for their heads, when the new emperor's army had no more use for them, that of Piso was given to his wife. That of Vinius was sold to his daughter.

Sold? To his daughter? How much would you give for your dad's dead head?

Super Spartacus

In 73 BC a gladiator called Spartacus led a rebellion in Rome. Who was he? He was from Thrace (which is called Bulgaria now) and originally he'd joined the Roman army. Then he'd deserted and become an outlaw. When he was captured he was forced to be a gladiator. He was so good he became a gladiator teacher.

Then he decided to go home and lead all his gladiator friends to freedom. Now, gladiators practised with wooden swords – they weren't allowed to use real swords until they went into the arena. So how did they make their escape past the Roman soldiers guarding them?

a) They went to the gladiator kitchens and pinched the knives.

b) They made their wooden swords really sharp and splintered the guards to death.

c) They put poison on the tips of their wooden swords and stabbed the guards.

Answer: a) Once they'd cut a few Roman soldiers' throats, of course, they could then steal the Roman weapons.

Spartacus' plot

Spartacus camped in the crater of the volcano Vesuvius – which, of course, was not erupting at the time. There was one easy path to the top of Vesuvius but around the other three sides there were cliffs. The Romans, led by Claudius Glaber, were happy…

All the Romans had to do was march up the path and attack the rebel gladiators.

If you were Spartacus, what would you do? (Clue: vines are very tough climbing plants with branches like rope.) Well? Are you as clever as Spartacus?

Here's what he did:

- His men cut the vines and made them into long ladders.
- They threw the ladders over the cliffs and all but one of them climbed out of the crater.
- The last man threw his weapon down and then climbed down himself.
- The gladiators walked round to the bottom of the one path so they came at the Romans from behind – where the Romans weren't expecting them.
- The gladiators attacked the Romans, beat them and captured their camp and their weapons.

Plutarch wrote...

> And now Spartacus was joined by farmers and shepherds of those parts, all tough men and fast on their feet. Some of these were armed as soldiers and some were used as spies.

Of course, the weapons came from the careless Romans. Spartacus had a real army now, not just a bunch of bandits. Big mistake, Claudius Glaber!

Spartacus' revenge

One of Spartacus' jobs as a gladiator had been to fight at funeral games. When he won a battle against a Roman general he gave him a great funeral – he made the Roman prisoners fight to the death. It was his way of taking revenge.

Suffering Spartacus

But in the end Spartacus' slave army couldn't beat General Crassus and his huge Roman army – it took ten legions (about 60,000 men) to beat the rebels. Six thousand of Spartacus' rebels were captured and all of them were crucified. Crassus placed the crosses at the sides of the main road into Rome as a lesson.

RUTHLESS ROMAN QUIZ

The Romans could be nasty – and so can *you*! All you have to do is turn off your television and hide the remote control. Then say to your foul family, 'Right! You don't get the telly back unless you get at least five of these foul Roman facts correct!' That's ruthless. Here are the questions…

1 What did King Tarquinius Priscus do to people who committed suicide?
a) eat them
b) crucify them
c) play football with their heads

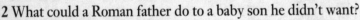

... AND TARQUINIUS GOES AHEAD WITH A HEADED HEAD!

2 What could a Roman father do to a baby son he didn't want?
a) leave it outside the city to die
b) throw it in the river to swim for its life
c) feed it to the family dogs

3 What dangerous game would some Romans try for a bet?
a) boxing with a bear
b) swimming with piranhas
c) running with their shirt on fire

BYE BYE

4 What would toilet cleaners do with the poo they collected?
a) sell it
b) eat it
c) tip it in a bog

5 When a traitor was beheaded in Rome, what happened to his head?

a) it was stuck on a spike

b) it was thrown into the sewers

c) its brains were eaten by the emperor

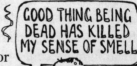

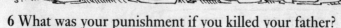

6 What was your punishment if you killed your father?

a) you'd get the sack

b) you'd be eaten by an elephant

c) you'd be strangled by your mother

7 Why did the Romans have trouble burying the traitors Drusus and Nero?

a) because they weren't dead and kept digging their way out of the grave

b) because they were so fat they couldn't find any coffins that were big enough

c) because they'd been chopped into so many small pieces

8 Rome was able to grow to be a great city because of its sewers. How big were they?

a) big enough for a man to crawl through

b) big enough for a 12-year-old boy to walk through without bending

c) big enough for a horse and cart with a load of hay to drive through

9 Romans fought and raced in an 'arena'. The word 'arena' meant 'sand'. Why was there sand in the arena?

a) to soak up all the blood

b) so it was soft for fighters to fall on

c) so fighters could pick up a handful and throw it in an enemy's eyes

THAT REALLY IS SOFT

10 What terrible torture did the Romans sometimes use on Christian women?

a) they tied them to a post and tickled them with giant ostrich feathers

b) they put them in a catapult and flung them high in the air

c) they hung them from a post by their long hair

Answers:

1b) King Tarquinius made poor Romans work on digging out the sewers for the city. It was back-breaking work. Many workers decided to kill themselves rather than get out of bed to go to work. (Even today a lot of people feel the same about work.) The King said, 'These people must not rest peacefully in their graves. Crucify them so the others can see what will happen if they commit suicide. Let them see the crows peck out their eyes and rats tear their flesh!' Nice man.

2 Usually **a)**. A Roman father had the power of life and death over his children. If he decided he couldn't afford to feed a new baby, he would leave it out to be saved by someone else, or die. But many Roman babies were thrown to dogs or drowned, or killed and then put on the city rubbish dump. Most of those babies were probably girls – worth less than Roman boys.

3c) Wearing a flaming tunic was a punishment for criminals. But sometimes Romans would wear one of those tunics and bet they could run, say, 100 metres before tearing it off. (Don't tell your teachers about this or they may decide to try that game at the next school sports day.)

4a) Not everyone was connected to Rome's wonderful sewers. Many houses let their toilet waste drain into a deep pit. But in time the pit filled with poo. Toilet cleaners would shovel it out, load it on carts and take it to sell to farmers. The farmers would spread it on their fields to help their crops grow.

5b) The idea was that you couldn't get into heaven if your head wasn't buried with your body – the gods couldn't have a lot of headless people wandering round, could they? But your body would be thrown in the River Tiber – and the sewers flowed into the same river. So there was just a chance your head and body could get back together! (All right, not much of a chance.)

63

6a) The 'sack' was a punishment for someone who killed a parent. Emperor Claudius loved to watch this form of execution. Claudius sacked more people than any other emperor. The murderer was sewn into a leather sack and thrown into the river to drown. Often there would be a snake, a monkey, a dog and a cockerel sewn in with the victim so they were clawed and bitten by the terrified animals on the way.

7c) Two brothers, Nero and Drusus, were accused of plotting against their great-uncle, Emperor Tiberius. Nero killed himself, but Drusus was shut in the palace cellars and left to starve to death. The brothers were cut into lots of little pieces. In fact there were so many pieces the palace guards had trouble collecting all the bits to bury them!

8c) In 33 BC the Roman General Agrippa had them cleaned out. Agrippa was also an admiral of the navy. His greatest boat trip was to sail through the sewers to check that they were clean. What a way to check a job. That's what's called 'thorough'. Still, from time to time, the sewers did get blocked and the forum was flooded with sewage. You'd have to hitch up your toga and paddle through poo.

9a) The sand soaked up the blood – sometimes. But after very gory fights or animal massacres there were slaves sent in to scatter fresh sand. Still, the rotting blood must have smelled pretty awful.

10b) In the city of Tyre in Carthage, in the AD 400s, the Christian women were stripped naked and thrown into the air by the Romans. There was no one to catch them.

EMPIRE TIMELINE

In AD 14, Augustus Caesar, the first Roman emperor, dies. The next 400 years will see a mix of good and bad emperors – but mostly bad.

AD 31 Emperor Tiberius had retired to Capri island in AD 26 and left the country to be run by Sejanus – leader of the army in Rome. But Sejanus started bumping off rivals so he could be next emperor. In AD 31 Tiberius had Sejanus (and his two children) strangled.

AD 37 Cruel Tiberius dies. Romans are happy – little do they know the next emperor, Caligula, will be much, much worse! He lasts four years before they murder him.

AD 43 Emperor Claudius arranges to have a little island invaded. It is Britain – and the Romans will stay for 350 years.

AD 64 Claudius dies from eating poisoned mushrooms and nutty Nero takes over. In AD 64, a huge fire destroys much of Rome and Nero is blamed. He says, 'It was those Jews that follow Jesus Christ! Blame *them*!' The Romans do and start hundreds of years of cruel executions of Christians.

AD **79** Mount Vesuvius erupts and buries Pompeii in southern Italy. Plenty of suffocated victims for historians to dig up in later years.

AD **80** The Colosseum is built in Rome – a nice big place to murder criminals and Christians for fun.

AD **117** Emperor Hadrian finds he is fighting on all sides just to keep the Roman Empire together. He builds a great wall across the north of England to keep out the northern Celts – the Scots. (But they still get in.)

AD **161** Emperor Marcus Aurelius thinks the Empire is too big and decides to share it. This is the beginning of two Roman Empires – the East and the West. In time they'll fight each other.

AD **165** The armies in the East return with glory – and a plague. It sweeps through the Empire and kills thousands. The Empire will never quite recover its strength.

AD **200s** Barbarians start to swarm on Rome – Franks and Alemanni from the north, Goths in Greece and Persians in the Middle-East – where they even captured Emperor Valerian in AD 260. Valerian was then skinned alive and his skin put on display. And when they aren't fighting

Barbarians, the Romans are fighting each other – no one can decide who should be the emperor.

AD **300s** Emperor Diocletian sorts out the Empire but retires in AD 305. The Empire is split again – with two emperors. Of course, they fight. Constantine eventually takes control of the whole Empire. He is a Christian who ended the killing of Christians in the arena – but not the animal hunts and the gladiator contests.

AD **378** The Visigoths have run away from the horrible Huns – Barbarians living in eastern Europe – but the Romans are not too pleased to see them and try to keep them out, so the Visigoths force their way into the Roman Empire and become invaders.

AD **410** The Visigoths take Rome and then Rome is open to attacks from everyone.

AD **476** The last Roman emperor in the West loses his throne. His name, like that of the first Rome leader, is Romulus. Very neat.

EVIL EMPERORS

Augustus Caesar became the first Roman emperor. The trouble was he was a *good* emperor ... so the Romans thought it was a *good* idea to have them. But even when some bad, mad and sad men became emperors, the Romans didn't give up on the idea – they just murdered the man and got a new one!

Here are a few of the foulest...

Horrible Histories Warning: Some of these terrible tales were told by the emperor's enemies. There may be a bit of foul fibbing in some cases. Don't believe everything you read in a history book!

Tiberius (AD 14–37)

Cruel Tiberius retired at the age of 67 and spent the last ten years of his life on the island of Capri – an island with some useful cliffs...

Five foul facts

- Tiberius had his enemies tortured then thrown off the cliffs into the sea, while he watched. Just to make sure they didn't survive there were sailors waiting at the bottom to smash the victims with boat-hooks and oars.
- His sister-in-law, Agrippina, was banished to Pandateria island off the western coast of Italy and beaten so badly that one of her eyes was destroyed. She starved herself to death.
- Her son, Drusus, was arrested and locked in a cell to starve. He even tried to eat the stuffing in his mattress.
- Tiberius fell ill and the next emperor, Caligula, took the imperial ring off the finger of the dying man ... then Tiberius sat up and asked for food! The commander of

the guards went into the room. Instead of food he had a cushion with him to finish off the dying old man.

- Tiberius was hated – even though Rome was peaceful while he ruled. He was remembered in two words…

BLOOD-SOAKED MUD

Caligula (AD 37–41)

Caligula wasn't his real name. He was really called Emperor Gaius. But he was born in an army camp and loved to wear little soldier boots. The name for little boots was 'Caligula' and that became his nickname. But when he grew up he hated being called that and punished anyone who did. Mind you, he didn't like the name Gaius much either!

Five foul facts

- He made mothers and fathers come along to watch their children being executed. That was sweet, wasn't it? If you were executed you'd like your mum there, wouldn't you?
- Caligula had his chief animal-keeper flogged with chains, day after day. At last the man's leaking brains started to smell so Caligula had him killed.
- Caligula often made his feasts more fun by having someone tortured as he ate. At one dinner he brought in a slave who had stolen a strip of silver from a couch; executioners lopped off the man's hands, tied them round his neck and took him for a tour of the tables, with a sign showing what he had done to deserve it.

- Caligula had a very hairy body, like a goat. So you'd be executed if you said the word 'goat' while you were with him.

- Caligula shocked Romans because he loved to dress up. He dressed up as Roman gods like Jupiter ... that was silly but harmless. The Romans really gasped when they saw Caligula dressed in a jewelled dress as the goddess Venus. He even robbed the grave of Alexander the Great so he could dress in the dead man's armour and pretend to be him.

Did you know…?
A fortune-teller once told Caligula…

When Caligula become emperor he still had to take his revenge on the fortune-teller by riding across the bay without wetting his horse's shoes.

And in AD 39 he did it. How? He had a bridge of boats floated across the Bay of Baiae and joined by planks. He then rode across. It was two miles long. The next day he rode back in a chariot. But Caligula had used just about every boat in Rome. The owners of the boats (and lots of Roman shopkeepers) lost a lot of money because they couldn't trade for a week.

Claudius (AD 41–54)

Emperor Claudius enjoyed games in the arena, watching people torn apart by other people or by animals. But there was one thing he *stopped*. What?

a) a gladiator chopping the head off a swan because it was such a beautiful bird

b) hunters chasing a bull on horseback because the horses were getting hurt

c) a lion eating a human being because he thought it was disgusting

---

Answer: **c)** Most wild animals in the arena tore humans to death but they did not eat them. (It's a fact that wild animals rarely eat humans.) But one lion had been specially trained to eat human flesh after it had killed its victim. The crowd loved it. Claudius didn't – what a kind man! So Claudius had the lion killed ... well, not all *that* kind, then.

Nero (AD 54–68)

There is no doubt that Emperor Nero was mad. For a start, he told people he was a god and anyone who refused to call him a god ended up in the sewers.

Nero also used to enjoy roaming the streets of Rome, beating up men as they went home for dinner. If they tried to fight back he stabbed them and their bodies ended up in the sewers.

Five foul facts

- Nero loved singing and performing – but no one was allowed to leave the theatre, even though Nero went on for hours and hours. Historian Suetonius said…

But Suetonius didn't like Nero and that may just be a joke and a bit of a fib.

- Among Nero's most disgusting hobbies was to keep a 'glutton' – a monstrous Egyptian slave who ate everything and anything he was fed. It was said that Nero really enjoyed watching his glutton kill a human and eat him.

YUMMY! BAKED BEINGS

- Nero loved his wife, Poppaea, dearly – he had his first wife murdered so he could marry Poppaea. But his love didn't stop him kicking her to death when they had a row.
- Nero murdered his step-brother, two wives and his mother. But he didn't murder his teacher, Seneca. Instead he just told him…

KILL YOURSELF, BEFORE I HAVE YOU EXECUTED

Seneca cut his own wrists. You wouldn't treat your old teacher like that, would you? (Better not answer that!)
- When the army came to throw Nero off his throne it was his turn to commit suicide. But he made a mess of stabbing himself in the neck and a servant had to finish him off.

Did you know…?
Nero was a winner at the AD 67 Olympics – even though he lost! He rode in the ten-horse chariot race … and fell off. But they gave him the prize because: **a)** they said, 'He would have won if he *hadn't* fallen off' and **b)** they were so scared of him they didn't dare let him lose!

Vitellius (AD 69)

This emperor was famous for eating like a pig. He had four feasts a day and often tickled the back of his throat with a feather till he vomited – then he had room for more food. His favourite snacks were livers of pike fish, brains of pheasants and tongues of flamingos.

Even though he loved food, his enemies said Vitellius starved his own mother to death.

Domitian (AD 81–96)

Domitian took over when his brother, Emperor Titus, died, and people soon learned to hate and fear him...

Five foul facts

- Emperor Domitian was always afraid that someone would stab him in the back. So he had his palace walls built of polished white marble so they shone like mirrors. That way, he could see who was behind him!
- Domitian was touchy about his bald head. When painters painted his picture they showed him with long, flowing hair.
- One of his habits was catching flies, stabbing them with the point of a pen and tearing their wings off.
- He was just as cruel to humans. He hated Jews and had them hunted down and executed.

- The priestesses of the goddess Vesta were not supposed to have boyfriends but he suspected them of having lovers and had four women executed – the chief priestess was buried alive and the boyfriends beaten to death with rods.

Commodus (AD 180–192)

Emperor Commodus fancied himself as a gladiator and trained with them. But he only fought with blunt weapons against feeble opponents.

Five foul facts

- Criminals were sometimes given stones to throw to defend themselves in the arena. That was too risky for Commodus. The Roman writer Dio Cassius said...

He once got together all the men in the city who had lost their feet from disease or accident. He tied their knees together and gave them sponges to throw instead of stones. He killed them with blows from a club, pretending they were giants.

- Dio had a problem. He had to stop himself laughing when he watched Commodus strut around the arena pretending to be a hero. Dio chewed bitter laurel leaves to keep the smile off his face as Commodus pranced about, proudly holding up the head of his victim ... an ostrich. If Dio had laughed then Commodus would probably have had him executed.

- Fighting against Commodus wasn't a laugh for the gladiators, of course, especially the ones he used for practice. One gladiator fought against Commodus with wooden swords. The gladiator decided to make Commodus look good and he fell to the ground. So Commodus drew a *real* knife and stabbed the man to death. Even when he wasn't trying to kill his opponents he could somehow do it. Dio explained...

> When he was training Commodus managed to kill a man now and then. And he enjoyed making close swings at others as if trying to shave off a bit of their hair. But instead he often sliced off the noses of some, the ears of others and different parts of still others.

SNICK!
YOW
LOP!
OUCH

- In the arena, Commodus never shed human blood – he killed animals but only fought humans with blunted weapons. Shedding human blood would be a disgraceful thing for an emperor to do!
- Romans went along to the games to watch other people die horribly. But when Commodus was in charge the visitors sometimes found themselves dragged into the arena to be victims. Imagine going to a boxing match and being told...

WE'VE DECIDED TO GIVE YOU A GO!

Valentinian I (364–375)

Emperor Valentinian had a cage near his bedroom where he kept man-killing bears. For fun, Valentinian had victims thrown into the cage where the bears tore them apart. (At least, when I say 'for fun', I mean it was fun for Val, but probably not for the victims.) Kind-hearted Valentinian set his pet bears free after they had torn dozens of people apart.

Ending emperors

Being emperor could be a dangerous job. Lots of people wanted your throne – and lots were ready to kill you to get it. Of course, you had your own bodyguard – the Praetorian guard, who were the only soldiers living in the city of Rome. The trouble was that often the Praetorian guard *themselves* wanted to get rid of you.

Who could an emperor trust? Answer – no one! Lots of emperors met grisly and gruesome deaths...

Wicked wives

Some empresses were as bad as emperors, taking part in plots to murder their husbands, their enemies and even their own children. The first empress was suspected of killing her husband, Emperor Augustus, to make sure her own son became the next emperor. Writer Tacitus said she'd worked out a way to harm hubby – and get away with it...

Livia lived on. She died at the age of 86. Her son, Emperor Tiberius, refused to go to her funeral.

Getting it down the throat

Emperor Claudius became ill with diarrhoea … well, it's not surprising really. His wife had fed him poisoned mushrooms! She was afraid he would recover, though, so she came up with a new plot. The doctor went to Claudius and said, 'It would help if you were sick.' He then tickled the back of the Emperor's throat with a feather. But the feather had been dipped in a deadly poison. That finished him off.

Flying eye

Emperor Domitian's wife was part of the plot to kill him. An ex-slave was sent to stab him – but the first cut didn't kill the Emperor and he fought back, trying to gouge out the attacker's eyes. In the end the other plotters had to rush into the room and hack him enough times to finish him off. Very messy – and his bloody corpse was probably covered in flies who wanted to party.

Drained to death

Emperor Elagabalus was not a nice man. He said to the Praetorian guard:

I WANT YOU TO KILL MY COUSIN, ALEXANDER

But the soldiers, who rather liked Alexander, said:

GO TO 'ELL, ELAGABALUS!

He turned to the soldiers' officers and ordered:

HAVE THOSE MEN EXECUTED

But the officers said:

Elagabalus knew he had a problem ... his own soldiers wanted him dead – and he was surrounded by them. So he hid himself in a trunk and arranged to have himself carried out secretly. But he was discovered and ran for shelter – into a toilet!

A Roman described what happened...

> *Next the soldiers fell on Elagabalus and killed him in the toilet where he was hiding. Then his body was dragged through the streets and round the arena. The soldiers insulted the corpse again by stuffing it into a sewer. But the sewer was too small to take the body. They took it out and threw it from the Aemilian Bridge into the Tiber.*

The main sewer of Rome was big enough to take some bodies, though, and quite a few victims ended up down there among the poo.

Promise for the patient

Many Romans made wild promises when Emperor Caligula fell ill. They gathered outside his palace and carried banners.

The trouble is, Caligula got better ... and made the men keep their promises! The writer Suetonius wrote...

A man had offered his life but didn't kill himself. Caligula handed the man over to his slaves. They were ordered to carry him through the streets, decorated with holy tree branches and finally throw him into the river.

Did you know...?

Emperor Caligula was killed in a narrow passageway. So narrow, the guards who planned to assassinate him had to queue up to stick a sword in him. Some of them happily stabbed Caligula in his naughty bits.

Pleb pun

Miserable, grouchy Emperor Tiberius hardly ever gave the people games in the arena and they learned to hate him. So, when he died, they had a party in the streets of Rome. They wanted his body dragged off and thrown in the River Tiber so they chanted a little Latin joke, over and over…

TIBERIUM IN TIBERIM TIBERIUM IN TIBERIM TIBERIUM IN TIBERIM

You don't need me to tell you what that means. You do? Oh, all right. 'Tiberius to the Tiber'. It's a bit like Americans chanting 'Mrs Hippy in the Mississippi' or Germans singing 'Rhinos in the Rhine' or Egyptians crying 'Neil in the Nile!' or … Chinese calling 'Nancy in the Yangtse' or … oh, you can make up your own.

Not a great joke, but it's hard to be funny at funerals. Anyway, the plebs didn't get what they wanted. The soldiers burned Tiberius to ashes. And it's not easy dragging a pile of ashes with a hook.

Getting it in the neck

Commodus liked to act as a gladiator, but gladiators were often common criminals and the Romans hated seeing their emperor making a fool of himself.

Commodus set off to a great ceremony where he would be made a consul and wear gladiator's armour. That was too much for the Romans – a bit like a king going to be crowned dressed as a tramp. So his enemies fed him poison the night before the event – but Commodus threw up. In the end an athlete, Narcissus, was sent to finish off the Emperor by strangling him – just as though he were the common criminal he pretended to be.

He was buried at night and the government (the Roman senate) demanded that…

HE SHOULD BE DUG UP AND DRAGGED AROUND THE CITY LIKE A CRIMINAL. THAT'S WHAT HE DID TO OTHERS - LET'S DO IT TO HIM!

They didn't. Commodus was left to rest in peace – and four years later Emperor Septimius Severus made him a god.

A FEW FOUL FACTS

Yes, you too can learn these facts and repeat them at the tea table. Shock your aunties and disgust your grannies. (That's what they were invented for, isn't it?) Invite them round to tea and make sure you've got plenty of food on the table.

DELIGHTFUL, CHILDREN. HOW NICE!

Then tell them the following...

1 Did you know that Julius Caesar entertained the Romans with mock battles? In one he had two armies with 500 foot-soldiers, 20 elephants and 30 horsemen. So many people crowded in to see these games that a lot of spectators were crushed to death. (Squeeze a chocolate éclair till the cream gushes out as you say 'crushed' – and use red food-colouring to make the cream look like blood if you like.)

2 Did you know that in AD 80 Titus had games lasting 100 days? Nine thousand animals were killed in the fighting. Some of the animals were wild and some were tame pets! (As you say 'tame pets' pick up granny's cat and stroke it with an evil look in your eye.)

3 Did you know that in 355 BC the Romans took 358 captives from posh Tarquinian families? They took them to the marketplace, where first they flogged them then they cut off their heads. (A jelly baby would be good to use to show this horror. But don't use a sharp knife and cut yourself. Just tear the head off.)

4 Did you know that if a Roman owed a lot of people money they could all take a slice of him with a knife in payment? (Cut into a tomato and show how little slices can be hacked off – very messily.)

5 Did you know that the Romans had gladiator fights at their feasts? Nicolaus of Damascus said…

> *When they were full with food and drink they called in the gladiators. No sooner did one have his throat cut than the masters clapped with delight.*

(Follow this with a squirt of tomato ketchup. Hold the ketchup bottle close to your neck.)

6 Did you know that a Roman traitor would be thrown off a high cliff – the Tarpeian Rock? (Spread a good dollop of strawberry jam on a bun. That's what the victim would look like at the bottom.)

7 Did you know the Romans had wonderful sewers that flowed into the River Tiber? The fish fed on the sewage – and the Romans then ate those fish. So, really, they ended up eating their own poo! (Lick your lips as you spear a sardine with your fork and munch it.)

8 Did you know, a Roman emperor called Vitellius invented a pie made from the tongues of flamingos and the brains of peacocks? (Take a scoop of ice-cream as you say 'peacock brains' and swallow it while saying, 'Mmmm! Gorgeous.')

9 Did you know that Emperor Elagabalus was fond of eating camel heels? (Tricky one, this. You may have to pop to the supermarket and ask for a pack of deep-fried camel heels. Serve them with jelly and say, 'Have a dish of jellied heels!')

10 Did you know, the first Romans didn't use money – they used salt! (Take the salt cellar and pour it over granny's treacle pudding, saying, 'Here's that five quid I owe you!')

MARVELLOUS MEDICINE

Roman medicine was a mixture of common sense and daftness. Many doctors were Greek slaves who had been set free – because the groovy Greeks knew more than the Romans about medicine. Other men became doctors because they were useless at everything else they tried – a bit like traffic wardens today. And, like traffic wardens today, Roman doctors often hung around on street corners. They would try to attract patients…

The doctors followed drunks home from the taverns, looking for business…

It's said that the doctors even told rude jokes to the drunks to try to get them to part with their money…

87

Here are ten foul facts:

1 If you suffered from epilepsy then there was a gruesome cure…

GIVE HER A DRINK OF THE WARM BLOOD FROM A DEAD GLADIATOR. THE FRESHER THE BETTER

I'LL JUST POP DOWN TO THE ARENA THEN

2 In early Rome medicine was made and dished out by the head of the family, i.e. dad.

3 The first Greek doctor in Rome was a man called Arcagathus, in 219 BC. He was very popular at first. But he used to let a lot of blood out of patients as a 'cure' and that often killed them. He became known as 'The Executioner'.

4 The Roman surgeons had some simple painkillers for doing operations. In one operation they would drill into a patient's skull – but they did NOT use the painkiller for that!

NO PAIN, NO GAIN!

5 Romans enjoyed their public baths, but the sick and the well bathed together so they helped spread disease! Plus from time to time some plague would sweep through one of their towns – but the Romans often blamed poisoners, instead! (There *were* people in Rome who were paid to go around poisoning people. Men like Canidia, Martina and Locusta would take your money and bump off your enemy. Locusta took Emperor Nero's money and killed his brother, Britannicus.)

6 Cato was a Roman magistrate. He wrote down some useful cures that you may like to try on someone you don't like:

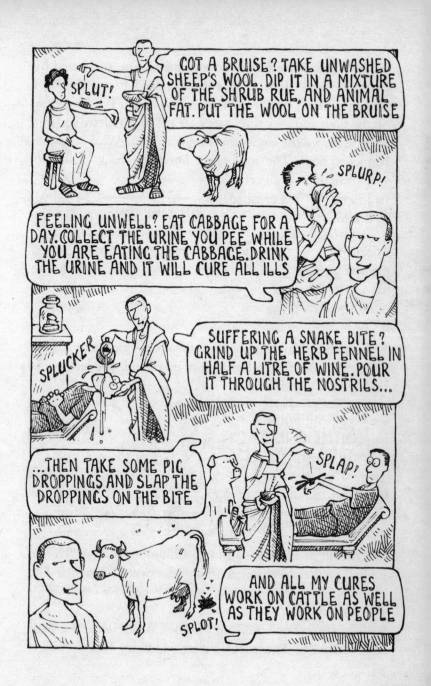

7 The Roman Diodorus had a twisted spine and hated his hunched back. Doctor Socles promised to set the back straight. (Don't try this at home!) The doctor lay the patient on the floor and took three stones (each over a metre square), then he placed the stones on Diodorus' back. What happened next? The good news: Diodorus' back was straight as a ruler! The bad news: he was crushed to death.

8 Emperor Caligula had a favourite gladiator called Columbus. But Columbus let him down and was defeated in the arena. Caligula said...

But the ointment was poisoned. Columbus did not live – if he had he may have sailed off and discovered America. But that was left to another bloke from Italy called ... er ... er ... I've forgotten.

9 Rome's most famous doctor was the Greek, Galen. But some of his advice to doctors looks a bit odd today. Galen said...

10 Galen was not allowed to cut up corpses. So he found out how the human body worked by cutting up monkeys (which are a lot like humans) and cattle (which aren't). That must have led to some mistakes…

AWFUL FOR ANIMALS

Want some fun in ancient Rome? Then kill an animal – or use an animal to kill a human. The Romans had animal-hunting games – 'venationes' they called them – in their arenas. Where did they get that idea from? Pinched it, of course.

Around 600 BC, an Etruscan drew a savage sketch. A blindfolded man, armed with a club, is being attacked by a dog. A masked man with a whip watches.

So what is going on in that sketch? It *may* just be an early example of the 'games' people liked to watch. Some historians say this is what the sketch means...

- The victim is blindfolded and thrown in a ring with a starving, mad dog.
- He can defend himself with the club – and even kill the dog – except he can't see what he is hitting. It's a bit like blind-man's buff with teeth.

- The man with the whip is there to make sure the victim doesn't run away.
- The dog dies or the man dies – either way the crowd has excitement and blood.

This may be an Etruscan idea the Romans borrowed. Other historians think the animal-hunting idea came from Persia. Persian King Ashburnipal used to massacre wild animals to show what a brave man he was. Sometimes he chased them in his chariot – but sometimes they were brought to him in cages. They were set free and the King then killed them while his people watched. Did this lead to this awful ancient joke?

FOOLISH SLAVE! WHERE IS THE GLORY IN KILLING A BUDGIE?

I GOT IT BECAUSE IT WAS GOING CHEAP!

Etruscan idea? Persian idea? Who cares? The result was still a lot of dead animals. And hunting, sacrificing and torturing animals certainly gave the Romans a lot of their fun. In Rome it could be really awful for animals...

Fiery for foxes

At harvest time it was a custom to catch a fox, wrap it in straw and set the straw alight. The flaming fox would then be left to run off and die in terror and agony. The Romans probably believed this would teach all vermin a lesson – 'Stay away from our crops or else this may happen to you!'

The custom may have come from a tale of a farm boy from Carseoli who punished a fox this way when he caught it stealing chickens. But the burning fox ran into a cornfield, set fire to the crop and destroyed it.

Evil for elephants

Elephants were great in battle. Send elephants charging at the enemy and they'll run for their lives. They were a bit like tanks – 2,000 years before tanks were invented and 2,000 years before this joke was...

The great general from Carthage, Hannibal, used elephants to scare the Romans. He also had a gladiator idea – he made prisoners fight one another and the winner would go free. This was to teach the soldiers of Carthage that death in a fight is better than death as a prisoner. Then one day he had a really bright idea...

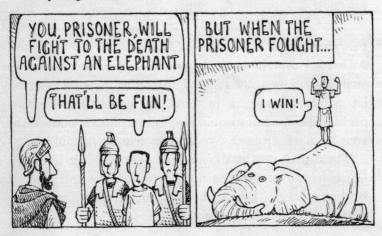

Rotten for rhinos

Most animals fought against gladiators or against other animals in the arena. Even if they won they were then killed by hunters or dogs. But some animals became favourites of the crowd. They fought bravely and the crowd decided they should live. One rhinoceros fought so well the crowd loved it. What did they do to this two-tonne terror?

a) They set it free. (It could cause a lot of laughs if it was set free in the marketplace!)

b) They ate it. (You get a lot of rhino-burgers out of one rhino.)

c) They sent it to fight again. (If he keeps winning he could be heavyweight champion of the world!)

Answer: **c)** The same rhino fought time and again in the arena for emperors Titus and Domitian.

95

Brutal for bears

Emperor Commodus saw himself as a brave fighter and a daring hunter. He liked to go to the arena and kill animals. In fact, he was a cowardy custard and never came near the animals in case he got hurt. At one show he had 100 bears put in the arena and then climbed on to a platform where the bears couldn't reach him. Then he threw spears or fired arrows till all the bears were dead.

You may think that is a disgusting and cruel thing to do – don't worry, most of the Romans at that time would have agreed with you. Commodus was murdered – and his sister may have been part of the plot.

Beastly for bears

A Roman leader in Greece gathered a large number of bears for an arena hunt. But the weather was so hot the bears died and were dumped in the streets. The poor people of the town came along with knives, carved up the animals, cooked them and ate them. Bears were supposed to attack people in the arena – but this time people ate the bears!

A Roman woman, the wife of Habinnas, ate bear flesh – and almost threw up. Habinnas himself said it was tasty – a bit like wild boar.

Gory goring

Wild boars were often put into the arena to gore victims with their sharp tusks. A really nasty trick was to tie a victim to the belly of a boar and let the maddened beast roll and kick and bite at the human. An animal keeper was tying a Christian to a boar like this when the boar used its tusks to gore the keeper.

Dreadful for dogs

In the reign of Emperor Tiberius a Roman called Sabinus was sentenced to death – along with all his slaves – for treason. But there was one loyal friend who wasn't put to death and stayed with him till the very end. His dog. Here's how the story goes...

There were a lot of witnesses, so this incredible tale of a faithful friend could well be true.

Lousy for lions

Emperor Caligula showed off his courage by entering the arena with a lion. Caligula carried a club – which was more than the poor lion had because it would probably have had its teeth and claws ripped out so it was no danger to the Emperor.

Of course it wasn't all lousy for lions. There is a famous story about a Christian called Androcles, a runaway African slave, who took a thorn from a lion's paw in the wild. Androcles was caught and sentenced to death in the arena; but he met the same lion in the arena and the lion refused to eat him. (Believe that if you like.) The Roman writer Apion said...

> *Androcles was set free and presented with the lion. Afterwards we used to see Androcles with the lion on a thin lead, going round the taverns of Rome. Androcles was given money, the lion was sprinkled with flowers and everyone loved to see them.*

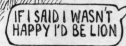

IF I SAID I WASN'T HAPPY I'D BE LION

What sort of flowers would you throw at the animal? *Dandelions*, of course.

The lion's tale

This is supposed to be a true story...

> Once upon a time there was a ferocious lion that hated men. He was fastened in a cage and longed to be free.
>
> From time to time men with whips came for him and chased him into a sandy arena. Thousands of human eyes watched him as he prowled and paced around the circle, looking for something to eat.
>
> Then he would hear the clank of a gate and the thousands of humans would raise their voices in a scream and he knew that meant it was dinner-time. He knew that some scrawny, scraggy human had been thrown into the arena and he would tear that victim apart.

Sometimes the victim knelt and prayed, sometimes they wept, sometimes they screamed and tried to run. But the end was always the same.

There was only one human the lion liked. His keeper. Every day the keeper brought him food and water and talked to him and stroked  him. In the stinking, gloomy, miserable cage it was the lion's only happiness.

Then one day the keeper didn't come. The lion lay on the damp, dark floor and sulked until men came with whips and drove him out into the scorching sun of the arena. On that day a bear and a leopard were there. (The Romans sometimes put in a few animals to kill the human and then watched them fight over the flesh.) The lion padded round and watched the bear and the leopard, and they watched him.

Then he heard the clank. The gate opened and the victim stumbled in. The gate closed behind him.

The lion was the first to leap. With huge bounds and gaping jaws he hurled himself at the man. Then a curious scent met his nostrils and he skidded over the sand as he tried to stop his final leap. It was the scent of his friendly keeper.

'Hello, boy,' the keeper said and the man's eyes were streaming with tears. 'My turn to be eaten, my friend!'

The lion growled.

'Go on. Get it over with. Make it quick!'

The screaming humans had gone curiously quiet. Even the emperor leaned forward from his seat and watched as the keeper stretched out a hand and rubbed the lion's mane. The lion turned his head and licked the man's arm.

Suddenly there was a savage roar and the man fell backwards. The lion saw the leopard leaping at the helpless victim. He threw himself between the leopard and the man. The furious leopard, starving and wild, lashed out with a powerful clawed paw but he was no match for the lion. The lion tore at the leopard and then had to turn suddenly as the bear scented the blood and lumbered towards them. The bear was powerful and his massive claws scarred the lion deeply, but the golden cat hung on till the big brown beast was dead.

The lion turned back to the keeper who was looking on in wonder. The emperor turned to the crowd and cried to them, 'What should I do with him?'

And the crowd roared back, 'Let him live!'

And so the keeper led the lion back out of the gate and his streaming tears were warm on the lion's scarred old nose.

THE END

Dreadful dinners

The wild beasts that ate people in arenas were expensive to train because they had to be fed with large amounts of fresh meat. They were trained by being fed on slaves. But there was always a danger the slave would fight back – and the Romans didn't want their precious beasts hurt by the slaves. So what did they do?

a) The slaves were tied up so they couldn't struggle.

b) The slaves were killed and chopped into pieces before they were fed to the animals.

c) The slaves had their teeth pulled out and their arms broken before being fed to the wild animals.

Answer: **a)** was not good enough because the slave could still bite the animal; **b)** was no use because the animals had to get used to chasing and killing live humans; **c)** was incredibly cruel – but that's what they did.

Emperor Caligula fed criminals to the animals – because it was cheaper than buying meat. He just lined them up, glanced at the prisoners, and gave the order: 'Kill every man between that bald head and the other one over there!' He also ordered that their tongues be cut out so their cries didn't disturb his peace and quiet.

PAINFUL PLAYS

Most people enjoy a good play – on television or at the theatre. The Romans didn't have televisions but they did enjoy the theatre. How did it start? I'm glad you asked me that...

The Romans showed their gods how much they loved them by having chariot races in their honour at their 'circus'. The people loved them and they were sure the gods loved them. But in 360 BC a terrible plague hit the city of Rome.

The Romans had more races – but the plague didn't go away. So they asked their Etruscan neighbours for help. The Etruscans sent dancers to perform in the circus. They became really popular with the Romans (and with the gods too, the Romans hoped).

MAYBE THEY SHOULD HAVE STOPPED THE RACES BEFORE THE DANCERS CAME ON

Around 200 BC, a man called Livius Andronicus added a story to the dancing – so it became a sort of mimed play. He pinched stories from the Greeks and soon the Romans had plays to watch.

In time the Romans wrote their own plays and began to mix drama with dreadful doings...

Theatre to make you throw up

You've watched murder stories, haven't you? But you know the blood is fake and the actors don't really get hurt at all. The Romans had a better idea. They would act out violent stories and, at the last minute, put a criminal on stage and *really* hurt him. It was real blood and real death the Romans wanted to watch.

- In some plays the criminal was dressed in golden clothes and had to dance happily for the audience. Then suddenly the clothes would be set on fire and he'd be burned to death. This sort of execution was called 'crematio'.
- A Christian writer complained that the Romans showed their gods on stage, dancing over the real blood and bodies of criminals. The god Attis was acted by a criminal, and the Roman audience watched as he had his naughty bits cut off – for real. The writer said that…

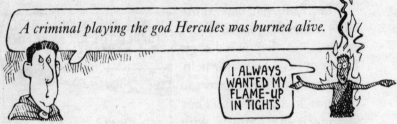

A criminal playing the god Hercules was burned alive.

I ALWAYS WANTED MY FLAME-UP IN TIGHTS

- The actors in Roman plays were often slaves, who might expect a beating if the audience didn't like them.
- Hardly any Roman playwrights bothered to invent their own stories. They just pinched them from Greek plays and wrote them in Latin.
- The Roman writer Terence complained that one of his plays was deserted by the spectators. They got up and walked out in the middle of it. Why?

a) The audience was disgusted because there was too much violence – they heard there was some peaceful music being played in the forum and left.

b) The audience was disgusted because there was not enough violence – they heard there was a gladiator fight to the death in another arena and left.

c) An actor fell off the stage and broke a leg – the audience couldn't wait for a replacement to arrive so they left.

Answer: **b)** Terence complained that this happened *twice* during his plays. Audiences rushed out to watch a tight-rope walker or a boxing match. If they grew bored with the plays they yelled out…

Maybe Terence should have written better plays, eh? Plays like this one…

Sickening scene

The plays themselves could be disgusting. In a scene from a story by Lucius Apuleius a gang of men talk about how they will punish a girl who's annoyed them. You might like to act this out in your next drama lesson – but make sure there is a sick bucket handy for the teacher…

Marcius:	I think we should build a big fire and throw her on it. Hear her scream and then hear her sizzle!
Festus:	Too good for her. Let's throw her to a wild lion and watch her try to run away.
Justin:	Where will we get a lion from, stupid?
Festus:	I never thought of that.
Marcius:	Let's skin her alive!
Verus:	Torture her, then hang her up by the neck.

Ferox:	No! Listen to me. All these are too quick. We want her to suffer.
Justin:	So what would you do?
Ferox:	There's an old donkey in our field and it kicks and bites and won't work.
Festus:	A bit like you, Justin!
Ferox:	Let's kill the donkey and take out its guts.
Verus:	I thought we were going to kill the girl!
Ferox:	I'm coming to that. We tie her up and put her in the donkey's belly. Then we sew it up with just her head sticking out.
Marcius:	That's good, Ferox. Then we put the dead donkey on a high rock in the midday sun till she roasts.
Justin:	When the wild animals start to tear the donkey apart…
Verus:	…they'll start to tear her apart!
Ferox:	And when she's almost dead we'll hang her from the gallows and let the dogs and vultures tear her guts out.
Festus:	Where do we start?
Ferox:	Justin and Marcius, catch the girl – Verus and I will kill the donkey!

(The men cackle horribly and leave the stage)

Nasty story. But the really horrible thing is the writer probably got the idea from some truly terrible punishments he'd seen in Rome. There are stories about two soldiers being sewn into the bellies of two oxen – while the animals were still alive! The soldiers' heads were left out so they could talk to one another and each see the other suffer. But some historians think that story may not be true.

You could perform this little play for your class during school assembly. But don't forget to tell them...

IF YOU DON'T LIKE THE PLAY YOU MUST GIVE US A GOOD BEATING!

CRUEL FOR CRIMINALS

The Romans didn't mess about when they caught criminals. Punishments were painful. Very painful. And many of them were made into shows for the public to watch.

Copy-cat crosses
The Romans liked crucifying people – nailing them to a cross and letting them die slowly. But they probably didn't invent crucifixion. The Persians had crucifixion first and the Romans thought, 'Oh, what a great idea! Look at how those victims are suffering!'

The Emperor Constantine ruled from AD 307–337. He banned crucifixion...

A wooden fork was built – the shape of a 'Y' – and the criminal's neck was placed in the fork. He was left to dangle there and choke to death.

Cruel Constantine

In the reign of Emperor Constantine (one of the 'kindest' emperors) there were over 60 crimes that could get you executed. He also invented a new type of execution … death by lead. Here's how he did it. *Don't try this at home.*

I. TIE THE VICTIM TO A POST

II. OPEN HIS MOUTH WIDE

III. POUR BOILING LEAD DOWN HIS THROAT!

As you know, lead is poisonous! So watch out when you chew those pencils!

Terrible Tiberius

Emperor Tiberius was definitely *not* a kindly emperor. A Roman nobleman had some coins in his pocket, which had the head of Tiberius stamped on them, of course. When the consul went to the toilet with the coins in his pocket Tiberius was furious! Having a pee in front of his face on the coins? How dare he? Tiberius had the man executed.

There is another story of a man who went for a pee at a banquet wearing a ring with the face of Tiberius on it. He might have been executed but a slave saved his life by stopping him from peeing!

Tiberius also had a man called Sextius Paconianus strangled in prison for making fun of him. But Sextius wasn't the only one who made fun of Tiberius. The sort of insulting things written about him were verses like:

He is not thirsty for good wine.
As he was thirsty then,
He warms him up a tastier cup –
The blood of murdered men.

Another poet wrote…

You monster! I'll be surprised, I will,
If even your mother loves you still.

Not surprisingly, perhaps, Tiberius had a poet called Aelius Saturninus thrown off the Tarpeian Rock for an insulting poem he'd written…

I SAID THAT TIBERIUS IS FAT.
I DIDN'T SEE MUCH WRONG IN THAT.
UNLESS I CAN FLY,
I'M SOON GOING TO DIE,
WHEN MY HEAD HITS THE GROUND AND GOES…

SPLOT!

Did you know…?

Tiberius made it a crime to change your clothes in front of a statue of the first Roman emperor, Augustus Caesar. (Mind you, these reports were all written by someone who didn't like Tiberius so they may not be completely true.)

Horrible historians!

In Rome it could be dangerous writing history books! Hermogenes of Tarsus was executed by Emperor Domitian for what he put in his history book. But the scribes who copied out the book for Hermogenes were also executed. They were crucified.

History writers today can get nasty letters, but those scribes got just *one* letter, a big 'X', and they were nailed to it.

Cutting comments

Emperor Caligula had people executed if they didn't enjoy the gladiator shows he put on for them. At one games Caligula brought a knight before him and accused him of picking faults with the show…

Pelted and pongy

Criminals were often executed quietly by being strangled in jail. But the most-hated criminals were executed in public so the Roman people could join in.

Emperor Vitellius faced a rebellion in AD 69 and lost. The rebels were coming to get him so he tried to disguise himself in rags and hoped his enemies wouldn't find him. But they did. The writer Suetonius described what happened next...

> *The soldiers tied his arms behind his back, put a noose around his neck and dragged him in his torn clothes to the forum. All along the way the crowds greeted him with cruel shouts. His head was held back by the hair as they did with common criminals. They pelted him with dogs' droppings. At the forum he was tortured for a long time then killed. His body was dragged off with a hook and thrown into the River Tiber.*

The Romans used hooks on hated criminals because they believed they were 'unclean' – no one wanted to touch their dead body.

Punish that person ... properly

Can you match the right Roman punishment to the right Roman crime? It would be criminal if you got too many wrong. So, anyone who gets less than four out of six can punish themselves by writing out 100 times: 'I am not verrey brite.'

1. STEALING CROPS

2. TELLING LIES ABOUT SOMEONE IN COURT

3. MURDERING YOUR WIFE BECAUSE SHE DRINKS WINE

4. SETTING FIRE TO YOUR NEIGHBOUR'S HOUSE (ARSON)

5. CALLING SOMEONE A NASTY NAME (SLANDER)

6. HAVING A BABY-IF YOU ARE A PRIESTESS

A. NO PUNISHMENT

B. WALLED UP ALIVE

C. CLUBBED TO DEATH

D. THROWN OFF THE TARPEIAN ROCK

E. BURNED ALIVE

F. EXECUTED BY BEING STRANGLED IN PRISON

Answers:

1f) Yes, throttled for thieving a few field things. (Try saying that fast with a mouth full of stolen cornflakes.)

2d) Of course, if you got away with the lies – and the man in court was executed – you would get all his money! Was it worth the risk? What would you do?

3a) That's right, one Roman who murdered his wife got away with it because, he said, she drank wine. Which reminds me of the ancient Roman joke…

4e) Yes, you'd be burned alive – after being whipped. This is a good example of Romans 'making the punishment fit the crime'. So, a pupil who flicks paper at teacher should be made to eat a book! (Without tomato ketchup.)

5c) Of course, you could escape the clubbing if the name you called someone was true!

6b) A priestess wasn't supposed to have babies but no one was allowed to kill one or the gods would be angry. So she was just fastened in a room (or buried alive) and left to starve or suffocate to death.

Dear oh deer

Romans often tried to make a punishment fit a crime. If you were a poacher who stole someone else's deer you may be sewn into the skin of the deer then set free. After a while hunting dogs would be sent after you. They would think you were a deer (because dogs are a bit stupid like that) and they would tear you to pieces.

YEUCK! WORST DEER I'VE TASTED IN AGES!

Did you know…?

People who were guilty of smaller crimes – maybe pinching food – could be sent to work in mines. But mine work was so hard and dangerous, they died anyway.

Lion in wait for Christians

Christians lived in Rome quite quietly until AD 62. They were a bit odd, the Romans thought, but harmless. Then Rome caught fire and a huge area was burned down. Emperor Nero said…

GREAT! NOW THERE'S ROOM TO BUILD THE PALACE I'VE ALWAYS WANTED

The Roman people heard about Nero's plan and put two and two together.

So an angry mob marched on Nero and he was in trouble. B-I-G trouble. Nero had to come up with a good story, fast, and he did…

The Romans decided to avenge themselves by killing Christians – and Nero helped a lot. He had the Christians rounded up, tied to poles in his gardens and covered in tar. When it grew dark he held a party in his gardens and, to light up the scene he had the tar-covered Christians set alight.

From then on the Christians suffered another 250 years of torture and death as emperor after emperor sent them to the arena to be torn apart by animals. There were many Christians who died bravely and their stories make grim and gripping reading…

Martyr meat
Thousands of Christians were torn apart in front of cheering Romans. But not all Christians were terrified at the thought. Some actually *wanted* to die because they thought it would be a quick and sure way to get to heaven.

One Christian called Ignatius of Antioch wrote…

> I am writing to all the churches, to say that I will be dying willingly for God's sake, if you do not stop it. Let me be eaten by the beasts. In fact, encourage the wild beasts so their stomachs may become my tomb. Let them eat all of my body, so no one has the trouble of burying me. I long for the beasts that are waiting for me. Or let them kill me with fire, and the cross, and struggles with wild beasts, cutting and tearing me apart, mangling of bones, crushing of my whole body, cruel tortures of the Devil; just so long as I may reach Jesus in heaven.

Brave man.

Pain for Perpetua

Vibia Perpetua lived – and died – in Carthage, North Africa. By March AD 203 she was married with a new-born baby. The region was ruled by the Romans and Vibia Perpetua was guilty of a terrible Roman crime – she was a Christian. Of course, that meant she would be thrown to the wild animals in the arena as many Christians were. All she had to do to avoid this was make a sacrifice to the Roman gods. She didn't have to slit the throat of a goat or chop a chicken. She just had to burn some scented wood – incense – and say, 'God save the Emperor.'

Perpetua refused. She went to prison with her slave, Felicitas, and three other Christian men, Saturus, Saturninus and Revocatus. She had a few weeks to write down her story in a diary…

When I was arrested, my father was angry with me but I stood firm. 'I am a Christian' I said. My father was so angered by the word 'Christian' that he moved towards me as though he would pluck my eyes out. But he left it at that and went away.

We were lodged in the prison; and I was terrified, as I had never before been in such a dark hole. What a difficult time it was! With the crowd the heat was stifling; then there was the extortion of the soldiers; and to crown all, I was tortured with worry for my baby there.

Then I got permission for my baby to stay with me in prison. At once my prison had suddenly become a palace, so that I wanted to be there rather than anywhere else.

The Christians were taken for trial in front of the Roman governor, Hilarianus. Perpetua wrote…

Hilarianus said to me: 'Have pity on your father's grey head; have pity on your infant son. Offer the sacrifice for the

> welfare of the Emperors.'
> 'I will not,' I retorted.
> 'Are you a Christian?' said Hilarianus.
> And I said: 'Yes I am.'
> When my father persisted in trying to
> dissuade me, Hilarianus ordered him to be
> thrown to the ground and beaten with a
> rod. I felt sorry for father, just as if I
> myself had been beaten. I felt sorry for
> his pathetic old age.

Perpetua and the three other Christian men were sentenced to die on the Emperor's birthday, 7 March. They returned to prison to wait. Meanwhile Perpetua's slave-girl, Felicitas, gave birth to a baby.

In prison Perpetua had a dream of a peaceful heaven and a hard battle against the Devil to get there.

> Then I saw an immense garden, and in it
> a grey-haired man sat in shepherd's garb;
> tall he was, and milking sheep. And
> standing around him were many thousands
> of people clad in white garments. He
> raised his head, looked at me, and said:
> 'I am glad you have come, my child.'

Perpetua was now looking forward to death. Another Christian took up their story on the day of the executions…

THEY MARCHED FROM THE PRISON TO THE ARENA JOYFULLY AS THOUGH THEY WERE GOING TO HEAVEN, WITH CALM FACES, TREMBLING WITH JOY RATHER THAN FEAR. PERPETUA WENT ALONG WITH SHINING FACE AND CALM STEP.

THEY WERE THEN LED UP TO THE GATES AND THE MEN WERE FORCED TO PUT ON THE ROBES OF THE PRIESTS OF SATURN. THE WOMEN WERE FORCED TO DRESS AS THE PRIESTESSES OF CERES. BUT THE NOBLE PERPETUA STRUGGLED TO THE END.

THE GOVERNOR GRANTED HER REQUEST. THEY WERE TO BE BROUGHT INTO THE ARENA JUST AS THEY WERE. PERPETUA THEN BEGAN TO SING A PSALM. AT THIS THE CROWDS BECAME FURIOUS AND CRIED THAT THE CHRISTIANS SHOULD BE WHIPPED. AND THE CHRISTIANS WERE HAPPY BECAUSE THEY WOULD BE SUFFERING THE SAME WAY JESUS HAD.

First in the arena was Saturninus who said he wanted to face several types of wild animal.

AND SO AT THE OUTSET OF THE CONTEST HE AND REVOCATUS WERE MATCHED WITH A LEOPARD, AND THEN WHILE IN THE STOCKS THEY WERE ATTACKED BY A BEAR.
AS FOR SATURUS, HE WANTED TO BE KILLED BY ONE BITE OF A LEOPARD BUT HE WAS FACED WITH A

WILD BOAR. THE GLADIATOR WHO HAD TIED HIM TO
THE ANIMAL WAS GORED BY THE BOAR AND DIED
A FEW DAYS AFTER THE CONTEST, WHEREAS
SATURUS WAS ONLY DRAGGED ALONG. THEN WHEN HE
WAS BOUND IN THE STOCKS AWAITING THE BEAR,
THE ANIMAL REFUSED TO COME OUT OF THE CAGES,
SO THAT SATURUS WAS CALLED BACK ONCE MORE
UNHURT.

None of the men were killed by the animals – the Romans would have to try again later. Then it was the turn of the women…

FOR THE YOUNG WOMEN, HILARIANUS HAD PREPARED
A MAD, HORNED COW. SO THEY WERE STRIPPED NAKED,
PLACED IN NETS AND THUS BROUGHT OUT INTO THE
ARENA. EVEN THE CROWD WAS HORRIFIED WHEN
THEY SAW THAT SO THEY WERE BROUGHT BACK
AGAIN AND DRESSED IN UNBELTED TUNICS.

FIRST THE COW TOSSED PERPETUA AND SHE FELL ON
HER BACK. THEN, SITTING UP, SHE PULLED DOWN THE
TUNIC THAT WAS RIPPED ALONG THE SIDE SO THAT IT
COVERED HER THIGHS. NEXT SHE ASKED FOR A PIN
TO FASTEN HER UNTIDY HAIR: FOR IT WAS NOT RIGHT
THAT A MARTYR SHOULD DIE WITH HER HAIR IN
DISORDER.

Imagine that! You are about to die and you are worried about your hairstyle?!

> THEN SHE GOT UP. AND SEEING THAT FELICITAS HAD
> BEEN CRUSHED TO THE GROUND, SHE WENT OVER TO
> HER, GAVE HER HAND, AND LIFTED HER UP. THEN
> THE TWO STOOD SIDE BY SIDE.

Saturus was brought back and attacked by a leopard that tore at him and left him bleeding.

> SHORTLY AFTER HE WAS THROWN WITH THE REST IN
> THE USUAL SPOT TO HAVE HIS THROAT CUT. BUT THE
> CROWD ASKED THAT THEIR BODIES BE BROUGHT OUT
> INTO THE OPEN SO THEY COULD SEE THE THROATS
> BEING CUT. AND SO THE MARTYRS GOT UP AND
> WENT TO THE SPOT AND KISSED ONE ANOTHER.
> SATURUS, BEING THE FIRST CLIMB THE STAIRWAY,
> WAS THE FIRST TO DIE.

But Perpetua didn't die easily. The Roman soldier was so nervous he hacked at her neck but failed to kill her…

> SHE SCREAMED AS SHE WAS STRUCK ON THE
> BONE; THEN SHE TOOK THE TREMBLING HAND OF
> THE YOUNG GLADIATOR AND GUIDED IT TO HER
> THROAT.

The Christians became 'martyrs' – heroes and heroines who died so bravely they made thousands of others want to copy them. Killing Christians in the arena didn't kill off the Christian Church. It only made it stronger.

Beaten but never beaten

The Romans enjoyed watching criminals being executed in the arena. But they seemed to hate Christians even more than robbers and murderers. Many Romans believed the Christians were cannibals. Sometimes games were arranged especially for Christian executions, and they often thought up hideous new tortures for the Christians before they killed them…

1 A Roman citizen who became a Christian, and was caught, was given a 'kinder' punishment than a common person. They would be beheaded. The common Christians were strangled in jail or thrown to the wild animals in the arena.

2 Death in the arena could be very slow – sometimes the Christians survived for days. Here's how the Christian writer Eusebius described some executions in Lyon…

Maturus, Sanctus, Blandina and Attalus were led into the arena and whipped. To crown it all they were put in a hot iron seat, from which their roasting flesh filled the audience with its scent. They were sacrificed after a day of suffering. Blandina was hung from a post as bait for wild animals to tear. None of the animals would touch her.

On the last day of the games Blandina was brought back. After the whips, the animals and the burning seat she was thrown in a net and shown to a wild bull. It tossed her to death but still the show was not finished. The crowd wanted to see the bodies torn apart.

3 The Romans made the living Christians suffer still further. They would not let their friends be buried, which meant that

their souls wouldn't go to heaven. Eusebius wrote this … but a few of the words seem to have been cut out of the script. That's the trouble with these old diaries. Can you put the words back in the right places to tell the terrible truth?

THE CHRISTIANS WHO HAD BEEN [ ] IN PRISON WERE [ ] TO THE DOGS. GUARDS [ ] THEM DAY AND NIGHT TO MAKE SURE WE DIDN'T HAVE THE BODIES [ ]. SOME ROMANS [ ] ANGRY CURSES AT THE BODIES. OTHERS [ ] AND MOCKED THEM. SO THE BODIES OF THE MARTYRS WERE LEFT [ ] FOR SIX DAYS AND THE REMAINS WERE [ ] TO ASHES.

The missing words, not in order, are: buried, laughed, unburied, thrown, screamed, strangled, watched, burned.

Answers: strangled, thrown, watched, buried, screamed, laughed, unburied, burned.

4 Christians were blamed for *any* disaster that happened to Rome. If there was a plague in the city then the Romans knew the answer…

CHRISTIANS TO THE LIONS!

5 Saint Lawrence was able to have a laugh about his execution. He was roasted on a grill over a fire. After a while he told his torturer…

I think I'm done now. Eat a slice of flesh and let me know if it tastes good.

6 The Christians drank wine and believed it was the blood of Christ. But they had other uses for wine too:

- In AD 265 the Romans burned Fructuosus and some priests in an arena. Their Christian friends took jars of wine to the arena that night and used the wine to put out the flames.
- At Ankara, in Turkey, Theodorus was executed. His body should have been burned to stop his friends burying it. But a priest took wine into the prison and gave it to the guards. When they were drunk the priest stole the body of Theodorus.

The more the Romans killed them, the stronger the Christians became. After all, the first Christian, Jesus Christ, had been horribly killed by the Romans on a cross. Many Christians followed him and died horribly – but that just made *more* and *more* people want to copy their bravery.

In the end the Christians won. There were so many of them they were able to take over and stop the horrors of the Roman way of life – and the Roman ways of death.

EPILOGUE

The Romans lived in savage times. They had better roads and laws and weapons and leaders than their enemies – the people they called the 'Barbarians'. And the ancient Romans are rightly remembered for their cleverness – so clever we can look back at their history and still be amazed. Look at their ruins and wonder how they built such great things as Hadrian's Wall or the Colosseum 2,000 years ago. Just don't be blinded by their cleverness. The real secret of their success was that they could be more savage than their cruellest enemies. Totally ruthless Romans.

The English poet Lord Byron (1788–1824) looked around the ruin of the Colosseum and wrote that in that place...

Murder breathed her bloody steam.

Spot on, Byron. Not 'games'. Not 'sport'. *Murder*.

Even today some of the best Roman ideas stay with us – but, sadly, so do some of the worst bits of ancient Rome. We'll never know exactly how many Christians were executed in ancient Rome – but it's certain that far *more* Christians lost their lives for their religion in the last half of the 20th century!

It's sad that some things never change. Humans can still be every bit as vicious as they were 2,000 years ago. Sometimes it's hard to spot the difference between the ruthless 1st century and the ruthless 21st century. Here's an example...

Case 1

A cruel ruler allowed no one to oppose him. One man who did struggle against the ruler was executed. As his corpse was thrown aside, the man's faithful dog stayed beside it and guarded it, heartbroken.

The place:	Ancient Rome
The cruel ruler:	Emperor Tiberius
The victim:	Sabinus
The dog:	Unknown
The date:	AD 35

Case 2

A cruel ruler allowed no one to oppose him. One man who did struggle against the ruler was executed. As his corpse was thrown aside, the man's faithful dog stayed beside it and guarded it, heartbroken.

The place:	Zimbabwe
The cruel ruler:	President Mugabe
The victim:	Terry Ford, a 53-year-old farmer
The dog:	Squeak
The date:	17 March 2002

The world changes. When will ruthless humans change?

MURDER, DICTATORS, BRUTAL CRIME AND LIONS

BOOK ON ROME?

NOPE. IT'S THE GUIDE FOR TONIGHT'S TV

More Horrible History…

The Rotten Romans

Follow the life of folks in Roman Britain with Brave Boudicca and the poor old peasants who tried to send the Romans back to Rome.

The Barmy British Empire

Discover the brutal facts about how Britannia ruled the waves – from infamous antics in India to dreadful deeds done down under.

Horrible Histories Special:

France

Packed with curious kings, quirky queens and evil emperors — and the rebels who had them butchered, beheaded and bumped off. Find out about France's foul famines, terrible Terrors and the gruesome guillotine.

Also available:

Cruel Crime and Painful Punishment

Meet 7,000 years of law-makers and law-breakers with a rogue's gallery of pirates, witch-finders, torturers, traitors and tyrants. And see if you can escape beheading in the terrible Tower of London game.